Dialogue & Initiative

2016 Edition

CCDS, the Left and the Progressive Majority

**Published by the
Committees of Correspondence Education Fund**

Changemaker Publications

Dialogue & Initiative is a discussion journal published by the Committees of Correspondence Education Find, Inc.,

2472 Broadway, #204, New York, NY 10025.

(212) 868-3773

Email: national@cc-ds.org
Web: www.cc-ds.org

Editors: Erica Carter, Paul Krehbiel, Harry Targ

Editorial Committee: Carl Bloice (1939-2014), Pat Fry, Michael Kaufman,Ted Pearson, Ted Reich, Meta Van Sickle

Layout and design for this issue: Carl Davidson

Manuscripts not exceeding 5000 words are invited. Send text via email; hard copy can be mailed or faxed. Manuscripts will be returned if a acompanied by postage-paid, self-addressed packaging.

ISBN# 978-1-312-21139-1

Order online direct at:
http://www.lulu.com/spotlight/changemaker

EDITORS' NOTE

With this issue of Dialogue & Initiative, CCDS finds itself at a crossroads as we approach our upcoming national convention. CCDS continues to do the good work we began 25 years ago.

However, despite some recruitment of younger members, the average age of our membership is increasing and our membership numbers are not. This has led to a discussion of proposals for how to move forward. This will be a major focus of our 8th National Convention, to be held in Emeryville, CA, July 29-31, 2016.

We have divided this issue of Dialogue & Initiative into four sections.

Section 1 presents a brief history of CCDS.

Section 2 reprints the papers and proposals that have been written during our pre-convention discussion period, many of which analyze our strengths and shortcomings and propose steps forward.

We apologize for the redundancies that appear in some of the papers, and the sometimes rambling narratives -- that is natural in discussion documents. We take an informed and reflective look at the future of CCDS as an organization and as a change agent in the Left Movement.

Section 3 discusses the work of CCDS, and the work we are doing with our allies in many of the movements for social justice and socialism.

Our Editors, from the top, Erica Carter, Paul Krehbiel, and Harry Targ

Section 4 addresses one of the most important issues of 2016, the presidential election campaign, and especially the explosive and inspiring campaign of socialist Bernie Sanders, and the right-wing threat posed by Donald Trump. The Sanders campaign has changed the national discussion from one of cuts, austerity, racism and social decay, to one of empowerment, jobs, education, health care, social justice and hope. We will have full coverage and analysis of the election campaign, our convention and youth school, and CCDS's future plans in the next issue of Dialogue& Initiative.

Table of Contents

Section 1. CCDS's History.

Section 2. CCDS's Future.

Section 3: CCDS's Work and Working with Our Allies:

Section 4. 2016 Elections.

Take a Free Subscription to Our Weekly E-Newsletter...

Easy to sign on and to unsubscribe as well. Go to http://tinyurl.com. ccdslinks, pick a back issue, and click the button in the left column. Arrives every Friday AM

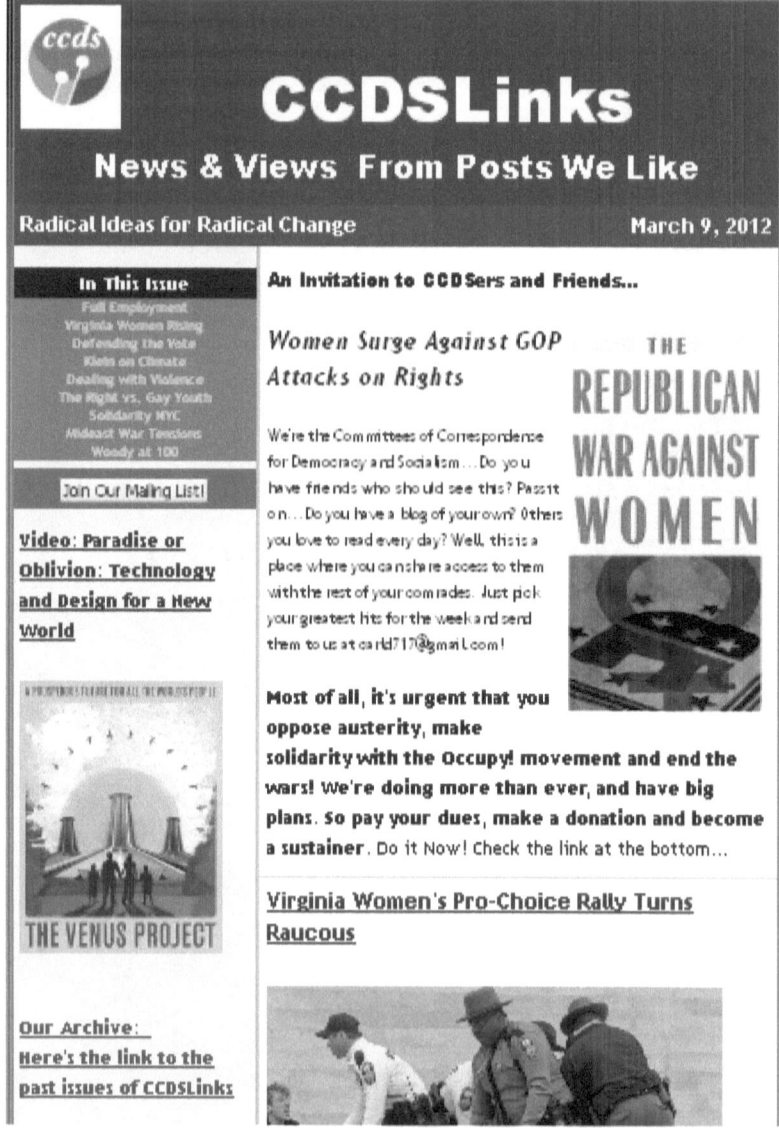

Section 1. CCDS's history

The Committees of Correspondence for Democracy and Socialism: A Brief History

By Pat Fry
CCDS Co-chair

Twenty-five years ago, the Soviet Union collapsed seemingly overnight, shaking the world socialist movement to its foundations. In the U.S., nearly a third of the membership of the Communist Party USA resigned in protest of an undemocratic, heavy-handed response to a call for a discussion of why it had happened. This was the genesis of the Committees of Correspondence for Democracy and Socialism (CCDS). As we approach the 8th National Convention of CCDS, it is worth a review of the organization's expectations and contributions since its founding. Though not an exhaustive history, it is hoped this overview will aid in discussion of the future of CCDS and the tasks of the left as the country faces an unprecedented far-rightwing bid for the White House in the November 2016 elections.

The Committees of Correspondence germinated at a rump meeting in December 1991 held outside the proceedings of the CPUSA convention in Cleveland, OH. A rigged election process had purged from leadership anyone who had signed a letter calling for an open discussion on what had led to the end of the Soviet Union. More than a third of the convention delegates walked out in protest and met to decide a course of action.

The meeting in "Room 211" across from the Cleveland Convention Center included some of the most important leaders of the CPUSA - Angela Davis, Herbert Aptheker, Charlene Mitchell, Mark Solomon, Jim Jackson, Kendra Alexander, Franklin Alexander, Barry Cohen, Carl Bloice to name a few. Participants took a collective deep breath and resolved to undertake a project for socialist renewal. Drawing from the history of the U.S. revolutionary struggle - the "Committees of Correspondence" was adopted as the project's name. A mass exodus of one third of the 3,000-person membership of the CPUSA followed.

Two months later on February 1-2, 1992, a meeting of the CP "dissidents" was held in New York City to discuss next steps. Some 28 local areas were represented - all had left the CP or were locked out of their jobs at the People's World newspaper, except for one who was a member of the Democratic Socialists of America. A wide ranging discussion was held on what the Committees of Correspondence should be. A network of mass activists? A new Communist Party?

A coalition of left organizations? It was decided that a wider discussion was needed to bring together activists of diverse political backgrounds. A national conference, eventually set for July 17-19 in Berkeley, CA, was decided. An Implementation Committee was elected - Carl Bloice, Barry Cohen, Charlene Mitchell, Joy Brock, Danny Rubin and Jay Schaffner - all former members of the CPUSA leadership. With only $3,500 in the bank, a budget of $85,000 was adopted. One full-time and one part-time staff person would be hired and an office to be opened in NYC. Charlene Mitchell who had organized the political campaign to Free Angela Davis was elected the Political Coordinator.

Perspectives for Democracy and Socialism in the 1990s - Berkeley, CA, July 17-19, 1992

Following five and a half months of organizing, the "Perspectives for Democracy and Socialism in the 1990s" conference was held July 17-19, 1992 in Berkeley, CA. Participation exceeded all expectations. With an initial goal of 350, more than 1,400 attended. There was much excitement and great expectation in the air. The hope was that the Berkeley conference would launch a left unity project for democratic, socialist renewal - a socialism that rejected dogma, orthodoxy and sectarian practices. Plenaries, workshops and meetings were held throughout the campus of UC-Berkeley. In addition to the many former CP members, a number of left organizations and publications were represented officially or unofficially - the Socialist Party, Democratic Socialists of America, Crossroads magazine, Solidarity, CISPES, National Committee for Independent Political Action, union members from the health care workers' union Local 1199 in New York, among many others. Individuals from the New Left party building movement of the 1970s participated.

Following the conference, an organizing committee met over the next two years to discuss and debate the shape of the new socialist project. The process led to the founding convention of a new socialist organization in July 1994 retaining the CofC name. The call to the convention was issued with a personal message from Pete Seeger, Ruby Dee and Ossie Davis.

Leaders of the South African Communist Party, the Brazilian Workers Party, and the Party of Democratic Socialism of Germany were guest speakers, associating the new organization with the worldwide movement for socialist renewal. A representative of the Cuban Interest Section delivered a message of solidarity from the Cuban Communist Party.

The founding document, "For a Democratic and Socialist Future," culminated months of debate. It outlined "goals and principles" that presented a coherent analysis of class forces in the aftermath of the collapse of Soviet socialism, and the importance of rebuilding a democratic and socialist left.

The Committees of Correspondence did not see itself as an end product but a bridge to a larger socialist organization rooted in the working class and mass social movements. The founding document stated:

"While we seek to facilitate strategic cooperation among existing left groups which share basic principles, we believe there is a need for a much larger progressive and socialist organization, one more reflective of the working class and oppressed communities and the radical democratic movements than any existing organization."

At the time of the 1994 founding convention, Bill Clinton had been in the White House for two and a half years. The assessment of the neo-liberal program of the Clinton Administration in the founding document was an example of the class outlook of the new organization. It stated that the Clinton electoral victory represented a defeat for the extreme anti-people policies of Reagan and Bush and his administration more responsive to popular pressure. It warned, however, of a growing long-term influence of neo-conservatism represented by the "New Democrats." Clinton's opposition to an increase in the minimum wage, the ending of Aid to Dependent Children, the policy of "workfare, not welfare," and NAFTA were examples. The statement called for a new political realignment, foreshadowing the center-left strategy of the "Progressive Majority" that would be adopted years later by the organization:

"We believe that what is needed is a comprehensive approach linking progressive currents into a broad, ongoing democratic force. We advocate a powerful, democratic political realignment, based on a new progressive social contract which empowers the masses of American working people."

The interconnectedness of class, race and gender was an essential component of strategy in the mass democratic movement and would become a distinguishing contribution of CCDS on the left. The founding document stated:

"The issues of oppression by class, race and gender intersect and their constituencies overlap. These movements must cooperate to achieve everyday goals, and they are joined by the common underlying objective of democratizing human relations in the personal, social, economic and political spheres."

A vision of socialism was set forth that demarcated itself from what the Soviet system had become:

"By socialism we do not mean a social system in which the state dominates everything, or in which authoritarian measures are used to restrict human rights. Socialism without democracy is not socialism at all." Rather, socialism "is a political, cultural, economic and ethical project, a struggle to transform power relations within a class divided society for the benefit of the overwhelming majority of the people. Socialism is not a fixed entity, but the social product of the dynamics of class struggle. Socialism must and will be constantly redefined by oppressed people who are engaged in struggle, over a long period of time."

Strategy Debate

The sharpest debate at the convention was on electoral strategy, a debate that continues today. Should the left support progressive Democrats? Should only third party candidates be supported? What is the meaning of political independence? Questions of strategy have been points of contention in every election cycle. Nevertheless, there was agreement on the following position in the founding document:

"We believe a strategic democratic alliance of social forces and movements is needed to effectively advance a broad progressive agenda. This should ultimately take the form of an independent, progressive political party. To that end, we work to build third party efforts, as well as forms of political independence inside and outside of the two main political parties, and democratic reform of our electoral laws."

Despite some differences and the diversity of political backgrounds, a new socialist organization was founded as a "work-in-progress." More than 500 people attended, and at least a third came from political backgrounds other than the CPUSA.

National co-chairs were elected that reflected the importance of class, race and gender as well as political diversity: Charlene Mitchell, Manning Marable, Leslie Cagan, Rafael Pizarro, and Sushawn Robb. Jay Schaffner was elected Treasurer and Charlene Mitchell National Coordinator. Thirty members were elected to the National Coordinating Committee (NCC). By-laws were adopted that reflected keen sensitivity to insuring democratic functioning. An example was the provision to elect half of the 30 member NCC at the convention and the remaining half by mail ballot vote of the membership following the convention. Additional NCC members could be added if a local chapter lacked representation.

The new NCC included 13 youth members with 4 named to the National Executive Committee (NEC) - Rafael Pizarro, Eric Quezada, Jonathan Peck and Gillian Young-Miller. A part-time youth organizer was hired in addition to one full-time and one part-time staff. A Youth Task Force formed and organized a conference in Chicago with 50 young people attending, committed to issues of criminalization, education and jobs.

Over 25 years, the Committees of Correspondence brought to its leadership ranks some of the most important leaders on the left. In addition to those named above, others were Arthur Kinoy, James Vann, Peter Camejo, Nathan Newman, Fred Hicks, Libby Frank, John Ratliff, Merle Ratner, Carl Davidson, Harry Targ, Mildred Williamson, Marian Gordon, Sandy Patrinos, June Hemmingson, Ed Hemmingson, Kendra Alexander, Franklin Alexander, Guiliana Milanese, Zach Robinson, Anne Mitchell, Fernando Fernando, Carol Lambiase, Carl Pinkston, Cheryl Richards, Manae Ross, Mael Apollon, Mike Stein, Jack Zylman, Kevin Bishop, Larry Abbott, Carl Bloice, Robin Busch, Jim Campbell, Barry Cohen, David Cohen, Edgar Cruz, Cindy Henderson, Tim Johnson, Ray Markey, Marilyn Albert, Barbara Blong, Howard Wallace, Roberto Ristorucci, Irving Beinin, Ann Ginger Fagan, Ira Grupper, Marty Price, Michael Kaufman, Van Gosse, Don White, Otis Cunningham, Mort Frank, Todd Freeberg, Maxine Orris, Walter Teague, Duncan McFarland, Gina Pesulima-Palencar, Will Jones, Karl Kramer, Ted Pearson, Jae Scharlin, Edith Pollach, Renee Carter, Kathy Sykes, Janet Tucker, Courtney Childs, Donna DeWitt, Mark Solomon, Will Emmons, Jim Grant, Jay Jurie, Paul Krehbiel, Jim Skillman, Diane Greene Lent, Carl Redwood, Ted Reich, Ellen Schwartz, David Schwartzman, Tina Shannon, Randy Shannon, Steve Willett, Meta Van Sickle, Denise Young, Attieno Davis.

The national office in NYC functioned with volunteers and paid staff that included Bob Greenberg, George Harrison, Bernice Linton, Ted Reich,

Mael Apollon, and Attieno Davis. (In 2013, the national office moved to San Francisco, and is currently staffed by Barbara Blong and Karl Kramer.) Local chapters were organized in over 20 cities. Regional conferences were held periodically on the West coast, Northeast, Midwest and the South.

Membership reached 1,971 by the time of the 2nd national convention held in July 1996 in New York City. Despite its growth in numbers, Charlene Mitchell noted in her opening address the lack of progress on a key goal of the organization - the "absence of a united and organized left that is able to exert major influence on the mass movements for social progress." The convention resolved to better integrate the CofC with broader progressive movements.

The Labor Committee held several face-to-face meetings and organized a national conference in Chicago to discuss strategy and tactics in the labor movement. The African American Task Force helped to build the Black Radical Congress, founded in 1998 in Chicago with 2,000 attending. The Living Wage Committee worked to assist and share experiences of living wage campaigns in several cities where members were actively engaged. The Peace & Solidarity Committee issued statements on U.S. military interventions and disarmament, helped to build the Pastors for Peace Cuba Friendshipment Caravans, and supported efforts to end the travel ban and embargo of Cuba. The Independent Political Party Task Force helped to mobilize for the Labor Party's convention held in Pittsburgh in 1998.

A Leadership Training School in July 1998 was organized over 6 days at a remote camp in Ossining, NY - 24 participants came from NY, North Carolina, South Carolina, Northern CA, and Chicago. This was the first of several schools organized over the years.

A Youth Conference was held in May 1998 in NYC where discussion focused on the problems with recruitment and retention of young people to the organization. They concluded that young people would be attracted to CofC if it had "clearer positions on and involvement in movements such as affirmative action and tuition inflation that have direct relevance to their lives." A youth magazine, called HX, was launched and Kevin Pranis was hired as editor. Despite the stated importance of work with young people, the inability to sustain membership of youth led to the eventual collapse of this important work.

In 2010-11, CCDS sponsored "Intergenerational Dialogues" in 10 cities, but did not result in any significant recruitment of young people to the organization. The lack of young people in the organization remains a critical weakness.

Differences Emerge on Direction

In August 1999, the 3rd national convention was held in Raleigh, N.C., signaling the political importance attached to the South. "In many ways, the South may become the pivot upon which we can turn this country around," said Charlene Mitchell in her opening address.

The Raleigh convention was a defining moment for the CofC. For its first five years, it functioned mainly as a network of activists involved in social movements. Grappling with the question of "What does the CofC do?" the NCC adopted a resolution earlier in the year to undertake Living Wage campaigns as a priority focus in the mass movement that would serve to recruit and build activist chapters locally. The CofC Living Wage committee published a pamphlet with model legislation for a federal living wage, and sought to coordinate work in local areas among members. A substantial minority of the NCC, however, disagreed and the debate was carried into the August convention in Raleigh.

At the convention, Mitchell argued that the CofC must act as an organized force. She reviewed the spontaneous struggles that had emerged over the past period and called upon the CofC to step up its work as a socialist organization. She noted the "sparks of resistance" to racist police killings, the "Critical Resistance" conference against the Prison Industrial Complex, the founding of the Black Radical Congress, and trade union efforts to win living wage ordinances in city councils, and said:

"As important - as necessary - as these are, they are not enough to bring about the type of social transformation that we - the conscious socialist left - want to bring about. They are not enough to change the power relations from capitalist domination to control by working people as a whole. They are not enough to bring about socialist transformation.

"To bring about a socialist transformation we need an organization that can take trade union consciousness, the consciousness of the nationally oppressed, the consciousness of women against their form of oppression and turn these into genuine class consciousness. That is, the type of consciousness that recognizes the interrelationship of these struggles and that the common enemy is capitalism.

"Is the Committees of Correspondence that organization? Only time will tell. But the CofC must have in its long-term outlook the importance of bringing such an organization into existence.

"In the meantime, we must decide on what type of organization the CofC is. In our short existence we have managed to hold our own in terms of membership...We have managed to gain the respect of many non-member activists and leftists...But to grow and expand our membership, we must resolve the problem of how to act as an organized force, not simply as individuals within an organization.

"The Living Wage campaign provides one opportunity to raise the level of activity of our organization...And it is an issue that can help define our organization."

After heated debate, the Living Wage proposal was defeated by the convention. The opposition argued against adopting one single issue as a priority when many issues were as important, such as halting the privatization of social security and public education. Others did not trust a national leadership body to decide priorities for local areas, a fear rooted in undemocratic practices of previous organizational experiences.

Another disagreement that had simmered since its founding was the view that the CofC lacked a well-defined political line and could not grow without one. The immediate task, according to this thinking, was a process to establish a new party. Mitchell argued against this approach in her opening address:

"There are some who say we need a revolutionary party...something beyond the CofC. They are probably correct. The question is, how is such a party brought into being? Previous experiences show that one cannot successfully declare a party by fiat. The material conditions for the development of a revolutionary party must be in place. The working class must be on the offensive. There must be growing unity between the potentially revolutionary forces of society. I don't think this country is at that point. What will bring us closer to that point is the successful functioning of a socialist CofC."

Engaging the Progressive Movement and the Left

Following the 1999 Raleigh convention, members of the CofC created an online daily news digest that would serve and build readership in the broad progressive movement well beyond the reach of the CoC. With a dedicated collective of moderators both member and non-member, Portside was launched in October 2000. The NCC adopted a motion to devote CCDS resources and staff time to building Portside, including the launch of Portside reader groups in local areas. Similar to the fate of the Living Wage campaign, there was significant disagreement within the NCC on a Portside priority and the resolution, though adopted, was never implemented. Portside moderators decided some time later to formally disassociate itself from the organization.

In 2000, a rightwing network commandeered the name of the Committees of Correspondence using a twisted interpretation of U.S. revolutionary history, similar to the Tea Party name utilized in later years. The CofC membership by referendum changed its name to the "Committees of Correspondence for Democracy and Socialism."

In July 2002, the fourth national convention was held in San Francisco, CA. Drawing from the large Bay Area left, some 450 attended. The September 2001 terrorist attacks and the U.S. invasion of Afghanistan fueled interest and discussion of how the left should respond. The convention program honored Rita Lazar who spearheaded the "Not in Our Name" campaign in response to the war-mongering use of her brother's death in the attack on the World Trade Center.

Speakers at the convention included Tim Wise, Elizabeth Martinez, Herbert Aptheker, Angela Davis and leaders of PDS of Germany and a representative from the Cuban UN Mission in NY. Cultural performances featured hip hop and spoken word young artists.

Following the U.S. invasion of Iraq in 2003, CCDS adopted a "peace and justice agenda" in advance of the 2004 national elections. It addressed "rising joblessness and falling wages, growing poverty and inequality" and the struggle against racism as a central requirement in preserving and advancing democracy. It called for a "new global policy based on ending military intervention, eliminating old and new weapons of mass destruction, and ending the blatant worldwide exploitation and misery embedded in capitalist globalization."

Trade unions and allies anchored a broad-based progressive coalition to get out the vote for John Kerry, a centrist Democrat who had less than enthusiastic support from the left. Weighing in, CCDS initiated a "Letter to the Left" calling for a united effort to defeat the right wing in the 2004 election. The letter was signed by more than 40 prominent left figures and endorsed by over 800 via an online petition.

Widespread ballot tampering and systematic voter suppression led to a second stolen election for George W. Bush. Responding to the prospect of four more years of a Bush-Cheney administration, CCDS launched what became a 4-year discussion of strategy for movement building to defeat the right wing. It took aim at discrediting the proposition that the Bush electoral victories of 2000 and 2004 represented majority sentiment. The facts on the ground and in polling painted a far different picture - the majority of the U.S. people were progressive-minded and could be won over to a people's agenda through the building of a left-center coalition.

The following summer of 2005, CCDS organized a major panel at the Boston Social Forum with Angela Davis, Bill Hartung, Manning Marable and Bill Tabb on U.S. militarism and corporate globalization.

In the fall of the same year, CCDS undertook to organize a broader discussion to engage the left on strategy. A day-long symposium placed the Progressive Majority strategy before a movement audience in December 2005 at the SEIU Local 1199 union hall in New York City. Speakers included Charlene Mitchell, Manning Marable, Angela Davis, Michael Honey, Damu Smith, and Chuck Turner. And, the event was covered by Amy Goodman of Democracy Now.

A second symposium on the Progressive Majority strategy was held the following year in 2006 in Chicago, the day before the 5th national convention of CCDS. Presenters included Angela Davis, Nation magazine labor journalist John Nichols, Sam Luebke, Deputy Organizing Director of the AFL-CIO, James Thindwa of Chicago Jobs with Justice, labor photo journalist David Bacon, and Rev. Calvin Morris, Jobs for Justice Clergy Committee in Chicago.

Notwithstanding the prestige of CCDS evidenced by the many movement leaders and thinkers that participated at symposiums and events, the organization was struggling 12 years after its founding. At the 2006 convention co-chair Mark Solomon said that while CCDS was held in high regard by the left and progressive movements it had not become a "vessel of organized re-groupment of various traditional socialist forces." Solomon laid out the key problem of CCDS:

"Our members, past and present, are busy in a variety of movements, but often confront this organization with indifference. We need to prove the importance of CCDS as worthy of time and energy. In short, we need to fight for this organization. There's nothing on the left quite like it."

In June 2007, CCDS sponsored two workshops at the US Social Forum in Atlanta. Following it, a Marxist educational retreat was held over 5-days for members of the NCC at the AFL-CIO's National Labor College in Maryland.

A week before, CCDS suffered a major blow as National Co-chair and founding National Coordinator Charlene Mitchell suffered a debilitating stroke. Mitchell's strategic leadership and accomplishments in the mass movement domestically and internationally were unmatched. Her role for CCDS has been irreplaceable.

In 2008, the election of Barack Obama as the first African American president was a watershed moment in the history of the country. It was a vindication of the progressive majority popular front strategy. Uniting the center and left on the basis of a broad based democratic agenda led to an historic advance in the fight for multi-racial unity and a major set-back for the rightwing centered in the Republican Party. CCDS leader Carl Davidson, with Bill Fletcher, Tom Hayden and Barbara Erhrenich, formed "Progressives for Obama," an initiative of left unity in the mass movement that played an important role in mobilizing the left in the elections.

The Obama election had fueled an optimism that permeated the pro-ceedings of the July 2009 third symposium on the Progressive Majority strategy and the CCDS 6th National Convention held in San Francisco. One of the featured panels was on building the progressive majority and left unity with representatives from the Communist Party USA(CPUSA), Democratic Socialists of America (DSA), Solidarity, and Freedom Road Socialist Organization (FRSO). Bill Fletcher and Steve Williams who would later become a founding leader of Left Roots also spoke. Veteran civil rights strategist Jack O'Dell was scheduled to speak but an illness pre-vented him from attending.

There was debate on the extent to which the Obama administration would or could carry out its promise to reverse 8 years of rightwing, neo-conservative rule. The convention was attended by some 250 peo-ple, much larger than the previous convention in Chicago, though the average age was 60 years or better. International guests of Die Linke (The Left) of Germany (formerly the Party of Democratic Socialism), the South African Communist Party, the Farabundo Marti National Liberation Front (FMLN of El Salvador), the Bolivarian Republic of Venezuela, and the French Communist Party spoke.

The convention adopted a new Goals and Principles document that spelled out the strategy of the Progressive Majority more fully draw-ing from the three symposia held from 2005 - 2009. The document ar-gued that the 2008 election of Barack Obama and the social forces that comprised his electoral coalition represented a realignment of political forces:

"The 2008 election was a blow against right-wing reaction that portends a left-center realignment of the nation's politics." The election of Barack Obama "was the response of a rising progressive majority that matured during eight years of neoconservative policies that represented the most reactionary sectors of U.S. capital."

In defining the social sectors of the Progressive Majority, the document stated:

"The multiracial working class in alliance with trade unions, women, Af-rican Americans, Latinos and other people of color, youth, and progressive sectors of business now form the promising components of the progressive majority. The profound challenge before the working class and its allies is to organize this majority into a coherent force capable of responding to the various issues it confronts."

The 2009 document analyzed the "free market" economic collapse of 2007-8, critiqued the "Crisis of Financialization" and "Capitalist Globalization," the war economy, the national security state, and the crisis of climate change. The main task, the document argued, was to build unity against the right and establish popular democracy. The Progressive Majority strategy was defined as:

"...the principal strategy to defeat reaction and place the country firmly on the road to progress. It is a strategy for building unity of the many currents of struggle" with the understanding that "the systemic basis of the interconnected crises of social life, the economy, climate and empire makes the solution of any one crisis dependent upon progress in solving the others. The unity of the many currents of struggle around these issues into a conscious progressive majority is a prerequisite to attaining sufficient power to establish popular democratic control of our society."

The complexity of the next 8 years under the Obama administration was anticipated in the document:

"The strength of a united progressive community is required to push back against the power of the financial sector, the military-industrial complex, and the pharmaceutical industry...Without counter pressure from the progressive majority, those regressive forces can be expected to prevail within the Obama administration. We will support progressive reforms by the Obama administration, including incremental reforms. Where the Obama administration continues past policies we will work with progressive forces to advocate a progressive agenda."

Lastly, the updated 2009 document made more concrete the vision of socialism and how it will likely develop in the U.S. Embracing more clearly Marxism as the defining politics of CCDS, it spelled out Marx's view of class struggle, the role of the working class, and:

"the inseparable relationship between the struggles of all nationally oppressed people and the struggles of the working class for a new society. We have an unambiguous commitment to the leadership of people of color and of women, acknowledging both the essential historical and current contributions of these groups to all major progressive achievements."

CCDS resolved to align itself with Jack O'Dell's 13-point Democracy Charter intended for use by the progressive movement in the way that the South African Freedom Charter had rallied democratic forces against apartheid. A Democracy Charter committee was established to help promote its use. In 2010, CCDS sponsored a workshop at the Detroit Social forum on the Democracy Charter with Bill Fletcher, Tim Johnson and Francis Fox Piven.

Following the convention, the NCC named Janet Tucker National Coordinator and Carl Davidson National Organizer. Co-chairs elected at the convention were Carl Bloice (re-elected), Renee Carter, Pat Fry and Carl Davidson. Mark Solomon and Jim Campbell became Co-chairs Emeritus. Steve Willett was re-elected Treasurer.

By the 7th national convention in July 2013 in Pittsburgh, PA, membership had fallen to 400. The national office in NY had been reduced to one-part time staff person. Youth were nearly absent from the membership. Finances were in poor shape.

Though the re-election of Barack Obama in 2012 was a defeat for the Republican right and a victory for the Progressive Majority, disagreements on this assessment surfaced in discussion of the main convention document. The convention referred the debate to a committee charged with writing a consensus resolution. The committee met several times in the following months but was unable to come to an agreement.

The Pittsburgh convention brought together 18 young activists for a 2-day school held in tandem with the convention. There were mainly from the South and a majority were African American and Latino. Two of the young participants joined CCDS and were elected to the NCC.

In October 2014, a fourth leadership school was held in NYC sponsored by the Carl Bloice Institute for Socialist Education, founded after his death from cancer earlier that year. A number of the young activists who attended the Pittsburgh school and convention were among those who attended the Institute's 2-day school in New York City. A fifth educational school will be held in Emeryville, CA. in July 2016 at the time of the 8th CCDS national convention, sponsored by the Carl Bloice Institute for Socialist Education.

Recent publications of CCDS include "Change the System, Not the Climate," a booklet produced by the CCDS Climate Change committee and distributed at the historic People's Climate March in September 2014. The Peace & Solidarity Committee published "Vietnam: From National Liberation to 21st Century Socialism," a collection of essays drawn from the experiences of U.S. activists on a study tour of Vietnam organized by CCDS. The Democracy Charter Committee produced a booklet, *"The Struggle for a Substantive Democracy: An Organizing Framework and Study Guide for Activists,"* highlighting the interconnected movements of the working class and the African American people.

The *Dialogue & Initiative* publishes annually and the *Mobilizer* membership newsletter is produced online every two months. *CCDSLinks* is a weekly news digest of politics and culture with 4,700 subscribers. The Socialist Education Project holds monthly membership-wide discussions via webex on politics, economics, and international developments.

The Online University of the Left (OUL) is a left unity project of CCDS with 7,650 subscribers and a core of 50 supporting faculty. As a unique socialist web portal, the OUL features video lectures, study guides, free downloadable books, archives and course syllabi. Since it was launched in 2012, over 70,000 individuals from around the world have visited the site at least once.

On Left Unity

The goal of building a "much larger progressive and socialist organization" envisioned in the founding of the Committees of Correspondence in 1994 remains largely still a goal. In March 2013, Co-chair Emeritus Mark Solomon spurred a national discussion on the left with an article published on Portside. He wrote: "The time has come to work for the convergence of socialist organizations committed to non-sectarian democratic struggle, engagement with mass movements, and open debate in search of effective responses to the present crises and to projecting a socialist future."

Three months later in June 2013, a Left Unity forum was held with live-streaming from a packed auditorium of SEIU Local 1199 in New York City sponsored by the Left Labor Project. Panelists were representatives of CCDS, CPUSA, DSA, FRSO and the Jacobin Magazine. Speaking for CCDS, Mark Solomon said:

"The quest for left-socialist unity is mandated by the maturing structural crisis of capitalism - with the gap between wealth and the rest of society widening to unprecedented levels. A resulting intensified class war, including an historic assault on labor unions, is driven in significant measure by a vicious right wing that is tearing at the fabric of social payments built up over 75 years."

Solomon proposed "...resolute steps at all levels to form unity committees as soon as possible, to forge united, concrete responses to austerity, to militarization and war, to ecological crisis and to launch the challenging process of building a socialist vision and consciousness. We cannot continue to drift with small, weak organizations resistant to change.... The present political and organizational status of the socialist left if unacceptable."

Notwithstanding the keen interest among many on the left, the organizations participating at the forum were unwilling to commit to forging organizational unity.

In February of 2015, Carl Davidson, Bill Fletcher and Pat Fry issued an 8-point program for left unity which was circulated widely with some positive response from individuals but no concrete organizational follow-up.

There have been more positive developments in local areas, however. The Left Labor Project, formed in 2009 in New York City has brought together left labor activists of CCDS, CPUSA, DSA and FRO to organize forums and undertake practical initiatives in the labor movement. In Los Angeles, CCDS, Solidarity and FRSO met over a six- month period to discuss left unity projects. A study group was initiated by CCDS, Solidarity and independent socialists on the intersection of the crises of energy, capitalism and the environment. In the Bay Area of California, the Socialist Unity Network (SUN) was initiated by CCDS with Freedom Road, Solidarity and others. SUN led to the organizing of an Eco-Socialist conference in January 2009, and the Oakland People's Climate March in September 2014 endorsed by nearly 100 organizations.

In 2016, the Boston CCDS chapter organized two left unity forums which then led to a day-long Socialist Unity Project (SUP) conference on April 30th sponsored by CCDS, CPUSA, DSA, Solidarity, Socialist Alternative, and others. The SUP will undertake an educational project and decide on a practical initiative in the mass movement.

Conclusion

The Progressive Majority strategy remains a solid framework for work in the mass movement. The multitude of grass roots organizations and movements - their growing structural cohesion and electoral manifestations - are promising developments. Socialism has had a more favorable standing as we see today in the response to the campaign of a socialist candidate for president. CCDS can play a role in providing a probing analysis of the system with education, particularly in the following ways:

1) Explain and advance the centrality of the struggle against white supremacy and against the increasingly oppressive and murderous role of

police and military - explaining why at this critical juncture in the development of global monopoly capital, systemic violence against people of color is growing and must be defeated;

2) Join with other left forces to build the broadest multiracial electoral coalition along the lines of the Moral Monday movement to pressure the Democratic Party nominee for President. The movement to elect Bernie Sanders should continue to capitalize on the efforts leading up to the Democratic Party convention and beyond through organizing at workplaces and neighborhoods. There are opportunities in state and local campaigns to promote candidates on the basis of a progressive agenda, utilizing the electoral arena as an important organizing tool.

3) Break down the fragmentation of the mass movement by advancing and linking together the Fight for $15, union organizing, immigrant rights, climate justice, anti-war, women's reproductive choice, Black Lives Matter, youth student debt, etc.

IMAGES FROM THE HISTORY OF CCDS

Committees of Correspondence for Democracy and Socialism

5th National Convention and Symposium
July 20-23, 2006
Chicago, IL

Fighting Back, Moving Forward: Strategies for Building a Progressive Majority in the 2006 and 2008 Elections
A Symposium of the Committees of Correspondence Education Fund
July 20, 2006   Chicago, IL

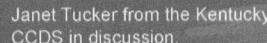

Janet Tucker from the Kentucky CCDS in discussion.

Rev. Calvin Morris, leader of Chicago Jobs for Justice Clergy Committee, and Mark Solomon, CCDS national co-chair presented views on "Connecting the Dots for a Unified Program for a Progressive Majority." CCDS Chicago leader Mildred Williamson chaired.

Rev. Calvin Morris

- We've got to respond in ways that speak to the broad center of people that are neither left or right.

- We are going to have to work with people who will not be as ideologically pure as we are, they will not have all the knowledge that we have.

- We have to connect the dots, we've got to mobilize, we've got to add to the numbers of people that are out there and willing to vote for change. The change that will come will not be an ideal one, but in words that are not part of my ministerial language, it will be a damn bit better than what we have now.

Mark Solomon

- Calls for a massive coalition built on a common program, leading to a common electoral policy, that would embrace both of the national labor federations, the new internet-driven organizations (ex. MoveOn.org), the major civil rights and peace organizations, women's movement, seniors, students and youth, gay and lesbian movement, etc.

- Within a broad coalition, there is a need for a large, effective left political organization that acts independently; an organization that consistently offers alternative visions on both foreign and domestic fronts. Historical example: Progressive Citizens of America until it was defeated in the cold war period in the mid and late 1940s.

- A new political realignment can only come from two directions: defections from the present two parties and the existence of broad independent forms.

The panel on "Connecting the Dots for a Progressive Majority" sparked discussion and an exchange of views on the content of the left-center coalition.

Some of the questions discussed: How does the left relate to the center? How do we define the left and center? Must the center adopt the positions of the left? Must the left submerge its agenda to work with the center? How does the left take strong positions, but at the same time leave the door open for movement, motion?

Where Have All the Jobs Gone and How Do We Win Them Back?

Carl Bloice, CCDS leader and journalist

"Where have all the jobs gone? That is easy to answer. Ford Motor announced it will cut 24,000 jobs in North America in the same week that a Chinese company announced plans to build a new plant in Oklahoma with 500 people.

"We need government policies that create new jobs. The U.S. is falling behind the rest of the world in green production – the development of environmentally sustainable products and services, like new mass transportation systems. "

Sam Luebke, AFL-CIO Deputy Director of Organizing

"Working people have lost power over the last number of years. Workers have lost the right to organize into unions.

"With the loss of union density is the loss of democracy. Unions are the forum that working people use to figure out how to respond politically. It is a forum for discussion of what is going on in the world and how to take action. At a non-union workplace, workers are scared, intimidated and divided and they don't discuss the issues of the day and their interests as a class."

David Bacon, photo journalist and author

"We need a strong coalition between immigrant rights groups, churches, unions, civil rights organizations, and working families that can build a movement powerful enough to win legal status and rights for migrants and jobs and living wages for everyone.

"Not only can we stop the rightward push but we can win something much better. It's time to fight for what we really want."

Angela Davis spoke during the box luncheon provided for Symposium participants.

"Community, it seems to me, is perhaps what we need most during this period, but community that is conscious, that is organized. Many people have wanted community without organization. They want an immediate community which is there so they can participate in it when they feel like it. It is possible to lead an entirely personal, private life and then decide on Saturday, I am going to be a part of the peace movement.

"This is an example of the extent to which our contemporary political activism seems to militate against long term organizational structures and goals."

Prof. Davis continued with a presentation of the relationship between the military industrial complex and the prison industrial complex.

Strategies for Winning at the Polls in 2006 and 2008

John Nichols, political correspondent for the *Nation*, described impediments to building a progressive coalition: gerrymandered congressional districts, the center/right stranglehold on the Democratic Party, media control by the ruling class, and a voting system that disenfranchises working class voters. In the 2006 elections, activists should target people under 30, single mothers who work at "Wendy's" and people living in rural areas.

Leslie Cagan, CCDS National Co-Chair and Director of United for Peace and Justice, said the Iraq war is a fundamental linchpin of Bush's foreign policy. She urged activists to connect the issue of peace to how the war affects the economy and jobs, health care, the environment and constitutional rights. And, she said, we must explain how people's lives are shaped by capitalism. The panel was moderated by Carl Bloice.

Committees of Correspondence Education Fund president and CCDS national co-chair Charlene Mitchell moderated the final "Summing Up Roundtable" panel.

James Thindwa, Director of Chicago Jobs with Justice, spoke about the labor/community coalition that was organizing a fight for a Chicago living wage ordinance. A few days later, the ordinance was passed in spite of vigorous opposition from big business.

Suzanne Adely, an organizer with the *Arab American Movement of Women Arising for Justice*, substituted at the last minute for Camille Odeh who was awaiting her daughter's arrival in Chicago after being evacuated from the Israeli bombing in Beirut.

It is a difficult time, said Adely, citing the Israeli assault on Gaza and Lebanon and the recent vote in Congress for sanctions against the Palestinian people. Yet, she spoke optimistically of the many "collaborations" taking place especially in the immigrant rights and anti-war movements with Arab American, African American, Latino, and Asian communities. "There are opportunities for movement building and change," she said.

CCDS 5th National Convention

James Campbell, National Co-Chair of CCDS and a leading figure in progressive politics in Charleston, South Carolina

In opening remarks, James Campbell set the theme of the convention arguing for the importance of organized, mass political action. He remembered the changes he has witnessed over his own lifetime, noting a transition from his private protest as a child, "cussing" grandmother, to mass political protest involving "correspondence" and activism.

Welcomes, Organizational Report and a 4-Year Review

Charlene Mitchell, National Co-Chair, welcomes members, guests, and observers.

Attieno Davis, National Coordinator, presents reports on finances, membership, and local chapters.

National Co-Chair Mark Solomon reviews CCDS over the period since the last convention in 2002.

A Socialist Vision

Mary Lou Patterson, M.D. reads an imaginary letter from a great, great granddaughter writing to her ancestor explaining what her socialist society looked like.

David Schweickart, author of "After Capitalism," offered his model of a society based on "market socialism."

Carl Bloice, member of the CCDS National Executive Committee and journalist, argued that a central focus of any new society must be the elimination of inequality.

Building a Socialist Left:
Connecting Class, Race and Gender

Howard Wallace, Founder of the AFL-CIO Pride at Work, a union caucus of gay and lesbian union members, San Francisco

Discussion centered on the necessity of the left to bring issues of inequality and discrimination into efforts to build a progressive majority. Issues that must be part of coalition work, they said, include living wages for home care workers, respect for people with HIV, and separation of church and state.

Mildred Williamson, Member of the National Executive Committee of CCDS

workshops

Economic and Social Justice

Participants heard from workshop leaders Rudy Lozano, Jr., a Chicago activist, and James Thindwa, Director of Jobs with Justice.

Peace and a Constructive Global Policy

Boston CCDS member and United for Justice and Peace activist Duncan McFarland co-chaired a workshop along with CCDS Philadelphia member Mort Frank who writes on issues of the military industrial complex.

workshop

Constitutional, Civil and Human Rights

Judge Claudia Morcom of Detroit had just returned from Geneva where she testified before a UN Commission on U.S. human rights violations. She reported on racism in the criminal justice system, discrimination against victims of the Katrina hurricane, and human rights abuses since 9/11 in Afghanistan, Iraq, Guantanamo and the U.S.

Organizing Youth, a Workshop of and for Youth

Jonathan Peck of Chicago's Southwest Youth Collaborative, and Angela Davis co-chair a youth workshop.

The workshop concluded that CCDS should make space for youth discussion and exchange. The convention later voted to launch a youth-only web page on the CCDS web site.

Independent Electoral Strategies for Building the Progressive Majority

Carl Davidson spoke about the importance of building independent electoral forms. He drew upon the experience of building the Chicagoans Against War and Injustice (CAWI) – established in the aftermath of the U.S. invasion of Iraq – into what is now a sought after voter registration and get out the vote block of independent electoral activists.

Ronelle Mustin, Vice President of the 22nd Ward Independent Organization in Chicago, talked about the importance of precinct organizing that builds a base of independent voters and activists between and during electoral campaigns. The 22nd Ward organization was a key base of support and organizing model for the mayoral victories of Harold Washington in the 1980s who was elected by a broad-based, multiracial progressive majority.

Culture, Youth and Hip Hop: An Evening with Poet Laureate Amiri Baraka

Panelists are Sam Lewis, of the Elastic Arts Foundation and SW Youth Collaborative; and Andrei Mills of the University of Hip Hop.

The overriding theme was the importance of art and culture in affecting social change.

Day of Internationalism

Helmut Scholz, Executive Director, European Party of the Left addresses the convention.

Charlene Mitchell reads a solidarity statement from the Consulate General of South Africa.

Socialist Mayor of Venezuela Addresses the Convention

Julio Chávez, the socialist mayor of Carora, Venezuela, a city of 300,000, and Martín Sanchez, Cónsul General of the Bolivarian Republic of Venezuela in Chicago address the convention, part of a U.S. national tour.

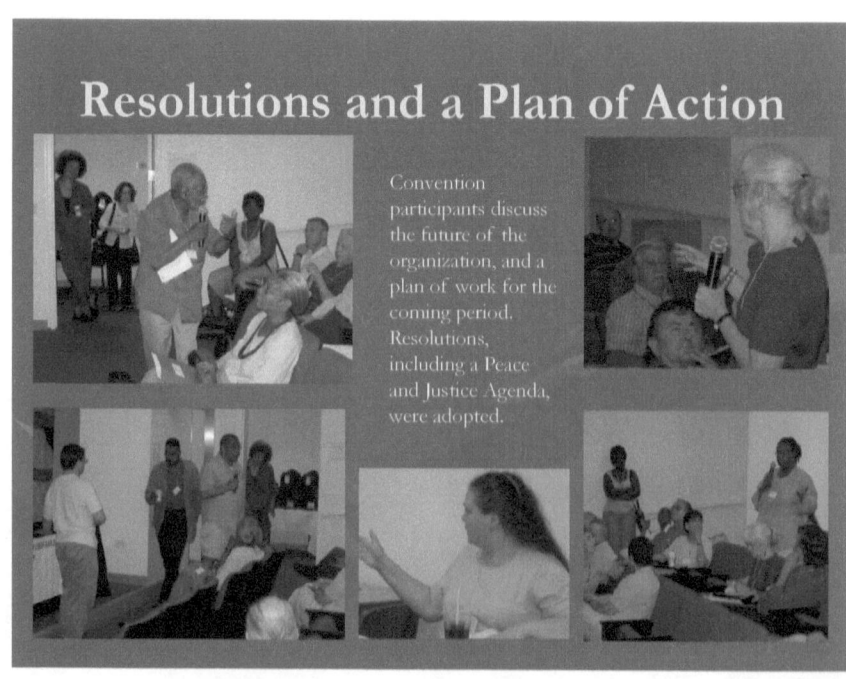

Resolutions and a Plan of Action

Convention participants discuss the future of the organization, and a plan of work for the coming period. Resolutions, including a Peace and Justice Agenda, were adopted.

Plan of Action for 2006 - 2008

Immediate Period

- Work with progressive coalitions to defeat the right in the fall elections, including support for the UFPJ "end the war pledge" campaign.
- Offer the CCDS Peace and Justice Agenda as a programmatic vision for the coalitions in which we participate.

Beyond November 2006

- NCC to initiate efforts to recruit young people and to develop and promote to leadership; create autonomous space for communication between youth and with CCDS, make space available for youth on the CCDS web site, facilitate one or more regional or national symposia to promote discussion on a larger scale.
- Establish a membership list serve.
- Establish sub committees of the NCC on Labor; Peace & Justice; Building a Progressive Majority;
- Chapter Building — rebuilding, beginning with report backs locally.

National Leadership Elected

National Coordinating Committee (convention)

Carl Bloice (San Francisco, CA)
Renee Carter (Alexandria, VA)
Carl Davidson (Chicago, IL)
Attieno Davis (New York, NY)
Pat Fry (New York, NY)
Marian Gordon (Los Angeles, CA)
Ira Grupper (Louisville, KY)
Duncan McFarland (Boston, MA)
Anne Mitchell (New York, NY)
Ted Pearson (Chicago, IL)
Harry Targ (W. Lafayette, IN)
Janet Tucker (Lexington, KY)
Meta Van Sickle (Charleston, SC)
Mildred Williamson (Chicago, IL)
Steve Willett (Oakland, CA)

National Co-Chairs

Leslie Cagan (NY)

James Campbell (SC)

Charlene Mitchell (NY)

Mark Solomon (MA)

Mail Ballot (post convention)

Marilyn Albert (Cleveland, OH)
Mort Frank (Philadelphia, PA)
Todd Freeberg (Knoxville, TN)
Ed Hemmingson (Albany, OR)
Fred Hicks (Louisville, KY)
Michael Kaufman (Oakland, CA)
David Makofsky (Oakland, CA)
Ted Reich (New York, NY)
Jae Scharlin (Berkeley, CA)
Walter Teague (Adelphi, MD)
Don White (Los Angeles, CA)

who attended?

Symposium

103 registered, 41 from Chicago

Convention

41 members in "good standing"

30+ non members attended one or more sessions
of the convention

3 joined during the convention

14 youth participated

Section 2. CCDS's future

Editor's Note: This section contains papers and proposals that were presented during the pre-convention discussion period and published on the CCDS website beginning in November 2015.

The 'Next Left' and the Tasks of CCDS

By Carl Davidson, CCDS Co-chair

From its inception, CCDS has seen itself as a transitional organization, a bridge to something larger, more inclusive and more effective as a political instrument for the US left in the 21st century.

We are now nearly over that bridge, and if you'll pardon my mixing metaphors, we are also now nearing the end game. The chess players among you will appreciate the point. Our forces are much reduced, and the end game is always very tricky. If you play it carelessly, coasting along, without much thought, well, you can easily lose. But if you play the end game well, you can still win.

What would winning look like in our 'end game'? Let's start with who we are. We have about 400 members active to some degree, and perhaps half of that fully active. We are largely '1968ers', veterans of the 'Long 1960s,' starting in 1958 or so and extending into the early 1970s.

This means we have a lot of wisdom and political experience under our belts, and that we are, for the most part, well embedded in mass organizations-trade union and civil rights, peace and justice, women and climate change, and so on. I won't do the whole laundry list, but despite low numbers, we are fairly well connected and embedded in the mass struggles. Demographically, we are also increasingly retirees. This frees up many of us to devote even more time to the cause. But it also means, to a great degree, some of us also reduce our level of activity and engagement-and it's only natural and personally healthy that we do so. Nonetheless, we don't have the same connections with a younger, rising generation, or social lives that bring us into regular contact with them, their groups and their debates and ideas.

In brief, I'm arguing that politics is largely generational, especially politics with revolutionary goals embedded in radical insurgencies. The main fighting forces today come from the Millennials, and we are increasingly on the other side of a generational divide to a degree that we can no longer discount. I'll also note here that we are not alone in facing this problem. The CPUSA and other groups largely made up of 1968ers face the same difficulties.

We have been well aware of this situation for some time. A few years back, we tried to organize 'inter-generational dialogues' in ten cities. We had mixed results. A few were excellent, others less so-but we made a good effort. For at least five years, we have also taken part in gatherings that draw in young radicals, like the Left Forum and the School of the Americas Watch, to engage in discussions and present ourselves with an upbeat public face, aiming to draw in younger recruits. We have created a number of valuable tools for radical education-the Online University of the Left, *CCDSLinks*, the annual publication of *Dialogue and Initiative* in an attractive book form, regular online discussion forums-and we have hosted or taken part in a number of 'Left Unity' gatherings and mass campaigns, like the Fight for 15, Black Lives Matter, and the Sanders campaign, largely comprised of younger people.

All this is to the good. But for us, it's still not enough. A 'next left' of 21st Century socialists is indeed emerging, but not quite as we planned or thought it might happen. Our major miscalculation was an assumption that we could draw these people to us. That, to be frank, with a few valuable exceptions, is not likely to happen. Instead, we are going to have to merge with them. That's the 'radical rupture' I'm proposing for our 'end game.' It was also the main conclusion Carl Bloice and I arrived at together in a discussion we had the month before his unfortunate passing.

So what should we do? Let's start with our aforementioned 400 members. What would be an ambitious goal over the next, say, three years? How about helping to pull together a nationwide left unity project with, say, some 4000 cadres? Obviously, this is not going to happen with us alone, or even mainly with us. But what would we want of such a formation?

First, that it be primarily made up of people from the 20 to 45 age range, i.e., the generation of our children and their younger friends.

(This comes from the strategic consideration that every revolutionary force in history is comprised mainly of the young).

Second, we would want it to be a full rainbow of nationalities, even a 'majority of minorities' as well as well-balanced gender-wise. (This come from the strategic consideration that the US revolution's main forces will come from mainly from an alliance and merger of the general workers movements with the struggles of the oppressed, especially people of color and women, i.e., the dimension of 'intersectionality.')

Third, we would want them embedded in the insurgencies of the young 'precariat' as well as having a foothold in more traditional trade unions and civil society organizations.

Fourth, we would want them to be flexible on electoral matters, willing to back candidates like Bernie, Kshama Sawant, Greens and even, in some cases, 'lesser evils.' (This comes from the strategic notion that history is made by the masses and of necessity of exhausting the battles for democracy, including the winning of government positions, and forming multi-class alliances, popular fronts, in the process).

Fifth, we would want them to love learning, to transform themselves into the 'organic intellectuals' and 'permanent persuaders' of a new Modern Prince, of a dynamic and disciplined 'militant minority' but a militant minority OF a progressive majority. (This comes from the deep connection between strategic alliances and the need for a core independent organization of the sector of the working class aiming for a new socialist order as well as immediate and transitional victories-the stronger the core, the broader the front).

The good news is that these forces are on the horizon, or exist in embryo, however you want to put it. The one with national reach is Left-Roots, which is working, city by city, to transform from a network to city-based cadre organizations. Another is the Boston Left Unity Project and NYC's Left Labor Project, where CCDS, CP, Solidarity, Freedom Road, Jacobin Readers and others are meeting and planning educational events. There are already more than 40 Jacobin reading groups spread across the country, and we are active in at least three of them. Still others are new local circles of Millennial socialists-Philly Socialists, Kentucky

Workers League, Appalachian Left, Louisville Socialists and others. They have been holding joint study retreats and conferences.

These young forces still have a long way to go politically (they don't always agree with each other), and are still largely disconnected organizationally. Forming a project of 4000 cadres out of it is doable, but difficult. I'm reminded of the problems addressed by some of our classic thinkers on the difficulties in overcoming 'the local circle mentality' and the 'mountain stronghold mentality.'

Even that 4000 would only be a small, first step. What the times REALLY demands of us is to turn that 4000 into 40,000, then 400,000. As distant as it may seem, the elements for it are right in front of our nose. If you add up all the participants in Occupy, Black Lives Matter (Occupy 2.0) and the Sanders insurgency (Occupy 3.0), and the Climate Justice mobilizations (Occupy 4.0), 400,000 is only a subset of all the people who have already turned out at rallies, making donations, or in the streets demanding radical change.

Our aim should be to merge our organization fully into these efforts of the 'next left,' locality by locality, as well as via any nationwide openings. We can still maintain our independence through our online standing committees, projects and publications. But our future is in bringing a new organization of 21st Century Socialism into being. We may be among its leaders, but we won't necessarily be in its dynamic core, which will likely be comprised of the best thinkers and fighters of the 'next left.'

This will require considerable discipline and collectivity, certainly on our part. We will have to break a lot of old habits and start doing things in new ways. The following list is only a modest beginning, but every element within it has an important reason behind it.

What we need to do

1.   Every CCDS member should get a Facebook account and an e-mail address, and a Smart Phone, if not a laptop with a webcam and headset as well. It is difficult to do social networking, online learning and rapid communication without these tools, especially across generations. (Consider what it would mean, in the 1920s, if you were a labor organizer, and didn't want to be bothered with a new-fangled telephone in your home.)

2.   Once on FB, every member should join the CCDS FB group and 'friend' the Online University of the Left, LeftRoots, Philly Socialists and others. Make yourself a user on the CCDS-Discussion.org site. Once you

gather FB friends, you should forward the weekly **CCDSLinks** to them- and send in emails to me for those open to getting it directly. (It's pitiful that we have these excellent resources that are largely not yet made use of by our members. When they are used, it is largely by people who are not yet connected with us in any organic way.

3.   Every CCDS chapter should have several people become LeftRoots 'Compas' and/or join or become supporters of local millennial socialist local circles that allow dual members. Our role is to promote unity and mutual learning in order to grow in the best ways. (We have to do this carefully. We want to present ourselves as resources, not as a domineer- ing force coming in to whip everyone into shape).

4.   Every chapter should establish at least one **Jacobin/In These Times** reading group for members, friends and new contacts. It should find ways to make use of the Online University of the Left in some of its ses- sions. (This is the most elementary way to meet, and as Charlene Mitch- ell often reminded us, if you don't meet, you don't exist).

5.   Every chapter needs a public face in its area. This can be a web page or a facebook group. In some cases, free local newspapers will do. If you don't know how to do it, we have a technology committee that will get you going. (How else will people learn about us? Word of mouth only goes so far, especially among the older generation. If you want to connect with younger people, these are a necessity, or you're not being serious).

6.   Every chapter needs to join or help form a Progressive Democrats of America or Working Families Party group in its area. If not PDA or WFP, it has to be a grassroots membership group with an electoral capacity. (The DC Statehood/Greens is one example) It has to be based on a plat- form of demands that can unite a progressive majority, not simply a mili- tant minority. This is an organic requirement if we ever want to see the progressive majority become a political player as a counter-hegemonic force. Otherwise, it can act from time to time, but it will always be under the thumb of a sector of finance capital and its candidates. For all the verbal importance our organization gives to elections and electoral poli- tics, it's shocking how little work we actually do in building independent electoral organizations of any type. I can count them on my fingers. And if we don't do this work ourselves, how can we ever present something concrete to a younger generation that demonstrates why it's important?

7.   While the tools of online social networking are invaluable, they only go so far. Understanding the important of face-to-face organizing and forming relationships from that work is valuable knowledge we have to pass on. But that means we have to get out of our own comfort zones at

times, and instigate public forums, 'happy hour' socials, debate watching parties and any other of dozens of forms that bring people together on a regular basis.

I'm sure there are more items for this list of tasks. But if we are going to play this 'end game' well, what matters most is how well we are organized. We can have the most wise politicians around, but without good organization, words rarely get transformed into deeds.

Responses:

Duncan Mcfarland said,

Hi Carl,

I agree with much of the first part of your essay. It's good to remind us of the original goal of CCDS: "From its inception, CCDS has seen itself as a transitional organization, a bridge to something larger, more inclusive and more effective as a political instrument for the US left in the 21st century." Today, we need to realize that the core of the leadership of the coming social transformation will not be the "68ers" but rather the main fighting force is now the Millennials. Our job is to contribute what we know and the skills we have, the positive aspects of 20th century socialism, to the younger generations who now are the majority and will eventually make the decisions on organization and program.

However, I don't find the goal of creating a national cadre of 4000 with huge demands on CCDS local chapters to be very realistic. If we haven't achieved that in the last 20 odd years, why would we now accomplish such an ambitious program? My approach is to build on the strengths that we already show. Thus we should connect, expand and promote a program of socialist discussion, analysis and education based on mass work. This should be a program priority for the next convention, along with a left unity workplan and a mass campaign such as opposing racism in different forms.

Carl Davidson replied,

Duncan:

The 4000 number was not meant to apply to CCDS alone, but to us working concert with LeftRoots and other Millenial groups. You're correct that it would be unrealistic for us alone.

Oftentimes bloggers and other pundits write stuff that if reexamined turns out to be ill-conceived and just plain wrong. However, looking at the essay below written after the 2014 election, I think it remains relevant to the struggles of 2016. Therefore I am reposting it. --Harry Targ

What to make of the elections - and what we should do next

Progressives must engage in education, agitation, and organization around social and economic justice issues while fighting the politics of fear.

By Harry Targ
The Rag Blog | November 5, 2014

I am looking at exit poll data and, as in prior election seasons, more Democratic votes came from the young, women, African Americans, Latinos, voters with post-graduate degrees and educational levels at or below high school, and low income citizens. This national polling data comports with results from many individual Congressional and state races. These groups of voters (or comparable groups of non-voters) will stay the same or increase as a percentage of potential voters in 2016 and beyond.

This data speaks to the necessary expansion of electoral and "street heat" strategies that prioritize several issues. Progressives need to continue to combat racism and sexism in all its forms. This translates into reversing voter suppression laws and other tactics to stifle voting, renewing the Voting Rights Act, pursuing equal pay for equal work legislation, opening the doors for citizenship to all migrants to the United States.

In addition, support for an expanded economic populist agenda is central to any progressive historical change. Candidates for public office should be pressured to support living wage legislation at the national and state levels, expand on worker rights to form unions, a green jobs agenda, revising the Affordable Care Act into a single payer system, and federal legislation (paralleling the United Nations Declaration of Human Rights) guaranteeing every worker the right to a job.

A program of social and economic justice should be basic to every candidacy in 2016.

This program of social and economic justice should be basic to every candidacy at the federal and state levels in 2016. To advocate for such programs, movements inside and outside the electoral arena should spend the next two years engaging in education, agitation, and organization.

In addition to struggles over concrete policies, progressives should engage more vigorously in ideological struggle. In general, this means addressing racism as a central undercurrent in American political culture: research and education that documents the centrality of the racialization of the 2014 election would inform discussion in the weeks ahead.

Also, a centerpiece of American political history, paralleling and sometimes overlapping with racism, is the politics of fear. The sources of fear in the past have included racial and ethnic others, foreigners, and communists. This election season fear was generated by half-truths about terrorists, particularly from the Islamic State of Iraq and Syria (ISIS), an invasion of Central American children, and a mysterious contagious disease traveling from Africa to the United States.

The politics of fear must be challenged, not accommodated.

The politics of fear must be challenged, not accommodated, introducing a politics of reason. That is progressives should demand that candidates address real issues rationally, demonstrate arguments using data, and to the contrary avoid simplistic sound bites. The people who need to be motivated should be treated with respect, including assuming that they understand their self-interest and can be convinced by compelling arguments.

Finally, campaigns opposing big money in politics need to continue. This includes the only short-term challenge to big money that has any chance of electoral success; that is organizing masses of people. In addition to increasing the struggles to build multi-issue mass campaigns, progressives can avail themselves of a multitude of media projects: alternative radio and television, free distribution newspapers, blogs, websites, and Facebook networks, as well as organizing study circles on college campuses, in senior centers, community centers, and public libraries.

I feel this morning the way I felt the day after Ronald Reagan was elected president. While the Reagan presidency institutionalized a neoliberal economic agenda that has shaped the national and global economy ever since, we also witnessed in the subsequent years the largest rally in United States history against nuclear weapons, a vibrant Central America solidarity movement, an anti-NAFTA campaign that almost defeated the passage of the treaty in Congress, various huge mobilizations against wars in Afghanistan and Iraq, and the election of the first African-American president in United States history.

Joe Hill was correct when he urged his comrades, "don't mourn, organize."

The Progressive Majority, Left Unity, and the Tasks of the CCDS

By Pat Fry
CCDS Co-Chair

This paper is offered for pre-convention discussion. The first section is a review of the history of CCDS and the "Progressive Majority" movement-building strategy. The second section reviews Left Unity efforts and its relationship to building the Progressive Majority. The final section is on the tasks of the left and CCDS as we approach our national convention in July 2016.

Section 1 "For a Democratic and Socialist Future"

"For a Democratic and Socialist Future" is the founding document of CCDS. It was the focus of discussions for two years beginning with a national conference, "Perspectives for Democracy and Socialism in the 1990s," held in 1992 in Berkeley, CA. The conference brought together over a thousand leftists from various political backgrounds. Many had recently resigned from the Communist Party USA in a struggle over democracy within the organization. Others had been members of various Socialist parties and many others were unaffiliated. Organizations sent representatives such as Solidarity, the National Committee for Independent Political Action, and the *Crossroads* magazine. There was an excitement about the possibility of launching a revitalized Left guided by principles of democracy and socialism, one that would "brush aside old barriers" and "develop constructive dialog on strategic issues and seek agreement on action."

A committee elected at the Berkeley conference met to chart a course for what became the Committees of Correspondence, founded in Chicago in July 1994. The "For a Democratic and Socialist Future" document was the defining goals and principles of the new socialist organization. It presented an analysis of class forces in the aftermath of the collapse of Soviet socialism, and the importance of rebuilding a democratic and socialist left in the face of capitalist triumphalism over the defeat of much of the socialist world.

When the CoC was founded, Bill Clinton had been in the White House for two and a half years. The founding document noted that while the Clinton administration was more responsive to popular pressure and his election was a defeat for the extreme anti-people policies of Reagan and Bush, the Clinton "New Democrats" represented a growing long-term influence of neo-conservatism. Clinton's refusal to raise the minimum wage, the ending of Aid to Dependent Children, "workfare, not welfare," and NAFTA were examples cited. The newly founded Committees of Correspondence called for a new political realignment in the country:

"We believe that what is needed is a comprehensive approach linking progressive currents into a broad, ongoing democratic force. We advocate a powerful, democratic political realignment, based on a new progressive social contract which empowers the masses of American working people."

A vision of socialism was outlined:

"By socialism we do not mean a social system in which the state dominates everything, or in which authoritarian measures are used to restrict human rights. Socialism without democracy is not socialism at all." Rather, socialism "is a political, cultural, economic and ethical project, a struggle to transform power relations within a class divided society for the benefit of the overwhelming majority of the people. Socialism is not a fixed entity, but the social product of the dynamics of class struggle. Socialism must and will be constantly redefined by oppressed people who are engaged in struggle, over a long period of time."

The Committees envisioned itself as a bridge to a larger socialist organization:

"While we seek to facilitate strategic cooperation among existing left groups which share basic principles, we believe there is a need for a much larger progressive and socialist organization, one more reflective of the working class and oppressed communities and the radical democratic movements than any existing organization. "

The Progressive Majority, a strategy for movement building

Following the second stolen presidential election of the Bush administration in 2004, CCDS - under the leadership of founder and national co-chair Charlene Mitchell - launched what became a 4-year discussion of strategy for movement building. It aimed to involve the broader left in a discussion on proving wrong the widely-held proposition that the U.S.

people in their majority were politically backward and reactionary. The facts on the ground and in polling data painted a far different picture - the majority of the U.S. people were progressive minded and could be won over to a working class, people's agenda.

CCDS organized a series of symposia sponsored by the CoC Education Fund to discuss movement strategy for uniting the key forces of the progressive movement, advancing an agenda and winning power. The first symposium was held in 2005 in NYC at the SEIU Local 1199 union hall with an all-day discussion that included Charlene Mitchell, Manning Marable, Angela Davis, Michael Honey, among a number of others. Two more forums followed in 2006 - one at the Chicago convention of the Committees of Correspondence for Democracy and Socialism (the name of the organization was changed in 2000) and in Boston at the first U.S. Social Forum. The fourth forum was held in San Francisco in July 2009 at the CCDS convention - six months after the country elected the first African American president on the basis of a center-left, anti-war agenda. The 4 year-long discussion culminated in the adoption at the 2009 convention of a revised "*For a Democratic and Socialist Future*" - also known as the *Goals and Principles of CCDS*.

The document argued that the 2008 election of Barack Obama and the social forces that comprised his electoral coalition represented a realignment of political forces:

"The 2008 election was a blow against right-wing reaction that portends a left-center realignment of the nation's politics." The election of Barack Obama "was the response of a rising progressive majority that matured during eight years of neoconservative policies that represented the most reactionary sectors of U.S. capital."

In defining the social sectors of the Progressive Majority, the document stated:

"The multiracial working class in alliance with trade unions, women, African Americans, Latinos and other people of color, youth, and progressive sectors of business now form the promising components of the progressive majority. The profound challenge before the working class and its allies is to organize this majority into a coherent force capable of responding to the various issues it confronts."

The 2009 document analyzed the "free market" economic collapse of 2007-8, critiqued the "Crisis of Financialization" and "Capitalist Globalization," the war economy, the national security state, and the crisis of climate change.

The main task, the document argued, was to build unity against the right and establish popular democracy. The Progressive Majority strategy was defined as:

"...the principal strategy to defeat reaction and place the country firmly on the road to progress. It is a strategy for building unity of the many currents of struggle" with the understanding that "the systemic basis of the interconnected crises of social life, the economy, climate and empire makes the solution of any one crisis dependent upon progress in solving the others. The unity of the many currents of struggle around these issues into a conscious progressive majority is a prerequisite to attaining sufficient power to establish popular democratic control of our society."

The complexity of the next 8 years under the Obama administration was anticipated in the document:

"The strength of a united progressive community is required to push back against the power of the financial sector, the military-industrial complex, and the pharmaceutical industry...Without counter pressure from the progressive majority, those regressive forces can be expected to prevail within the Obama administration. We will support progressive reforms by the Obama administration, including incremental reforms. Where the Obama administration continues past policies we will work with progressive forces to advocate a progressive agenda."

Lastly, the updated 2009 document made more concrete the vision of socialism and how it will likely develop in the U.S. Embracing more clearly Marxism as the defining politics of CCDS, it spells out Marx's view of class struggle, the role of the working class, and "the inseparable relationship between the struggles of all nationally oppressed people and the struggles of the working class for a new society. We have an unambiguous commitment to the leadership of people of color and of women, acknowledging both the essential historical and current contributions of these groups to all major progressive achievements."

The period since the adoption of the 2009 "*For a Democratic and Socialist Future*" document have confirmed its propositions. The Progressive Majority began to take shape organizationally at the national level with the "One Nation Working Together" mobilization in 2010 in Washington DC. This coalition was the first to bring leading forces of organized labor, the civil rights movement and the peace movement to the same table in protest of the rightwing Tea Party which had formed in reaction to the Obama presidency. Although the coalition was not sustained, an important outcome was the founding of the New Priorities Campaign, a peace and labor movement initiative to "move the money" from military spending to productive job creation and social programs.

The most important development to date of the Progressive Majority has been the Moral Monday movement that began in February 2006 with an NAACP-led coalition march on the state capital of North Carolina, called the HKoJ (Historic Thousands on Jones Street) March and Rally, in support of a 14 point People's Agenda. The multi-issue coalition has mushroomed into what became the "Moral Monday" protest of the ALEC-organized right wing takeover of the N.C. state government. The Moral Monday "fusion" strategy has joined together 150 coalition partners of organized labor, civil rights, teachers and students, housing activists, LGBTQ rights, voting rights activists, women's organizations. In the last few years, the Moral Monday movement has spread to several states in the South and Midwest bringing together civil rights and labor as the main anchors of this important cross-sectoral movement.

The civil rights unionism strategy that successfully organized industries such as the tobacco fields of North Carolina in the 1930s has once again become the blueprint for new industrial organizing campaigns in the South and elsewhere. "Union rights are civil rights" is the slogan of the UAW Nissan organizing campaign bringing together the African American community and student organizations of HBCU campuses in support of organized labor in Mississippi.

The People's Climate March of September 2014 in NYC broke new ground in uniting progressive forces and joining the struggles of climate, environmental justice, Native American rights, labor, peace and justice movements. Several months of organizing that consciously built unity among the various progressive silos resulted in an estimated 400,000 in the streets under a multitude of colors, banners and issues. This unity has become the hallmark of organizing in the months since that historic march under the umbrella of the People's Climate Movement.

On October 14, 2015, a National Day of Action on Climate Change saw protests in over 200 cities. In NYC several hundred protesters comprised mainly of immigrant worker organizations, Native American groups, trade unions, environmental justice and housing rights activists took over the street in front of Chase Bank in mid-town Manhattan. The issues of climate change, environmental justice, home foreclosures, and labor rights were joined together. In Miami, the labor-community coalition, Florida New Majority, organized the largest of the nation's protests with some 2,000 marching on October 14th.

Trade unions gave significant support to the 2011 Occupy movement throughout the two month long occupation of Zuccotti Park protesting income inequality and Wall Street greed. Significant sectors of organized labor joined with the Black Lives Matter protests of racist police murders from Ferguson to New York and Chicago. In the aftermath of the police killing of Michael Brown in 2014, AFL-CIO president Richard Trumka delivered a stinging speech in St. Louis on the history of the racism within organized labor and how it has divided the working class. The August 2015 protest march in Chicago organized by the Chicago Alliance against Racist and Political Repression to demand legislation for civilian control of police was endorsed and supported by several Chicago union locals.

The Fight for $15 strike actions of fast food workers that began in November 2012 in NYC have grown beyond what was ever imagined. The campaign has changed the national conversation on living wages and growing income inequality. Led mainly by Black and Latino young workers, the mobilization is now in its third year. The next National Day of Action on November 10, 2015 will see strikes throughout the country and is expected to be larger than the huge turnout on April 15, 2015. Significantly, it is no longer a labor-only struggle. Linking the issues and movements, organizers of the Black Lives Matter and Climate Change movements have been attending organizing meetings. NARAL has just announced support of the strike action and is organizing a contingent. It is expected that many other progressive movements will be joining the worker-led protests on November 10.

There is a new consciousness of the importance of a strategy to link issues and movements into an interlocking force, targeting a common enemy. This is only the beginning - CCDS and the Left must help to build and nurture this interconnected movement-building strategy.

Discussion on Strategy at the 2013 CCDS Convention

At the 2013 CCDS convention, there was discussion on a section of the main convention resolution that argued for "New Alignments, New Strategies." The debate was confusing, ill-prepared and inconclusive. Therefore, the convention voted to move the discussion to a committee that would arrive at a consensus document to be voted upon by the incoming NCC. However, the committee that was charged with this task was not successful; and, after four meetings it became clear that it was not possible to reconcile the underlying differences without a wider discussion in the organization.

The differences centered on replacing the Progressive Majority strategy with a "United Front" strategy. I argued then and continue to argue that the United Front strategy places a narrow emphasis on the working class and anti-capitalism. The Progressive Majority strategy sees uniting a range of class forces that will include sectors of small and big capital against the most reactionary sectors of capital in struggle for popular, democratic control of the country. It identifies the leading sectors of the multi-class, progressive majority as the working class, nationally oppressed, women and youth.

The July 2016 convention affords us the opportunity to further this debate. The Convention Program Committee may want to organize a panel discussion on the Progressive Majority strategy and opposing views. Strategy for Socialism?

The Progressive Majority strategy is not disconnected from the strategy for socialism. It is, in fact, a prerequisite for socialist transformation. The upsurge in the progressive movement must continue to grow and build organizational structures that can advance democracy on multiple fronts - the right to organize unions and collective bargaining, a new New Deal jobs program, the right to democratic control of police departments, the end of policies of mass incarceration, the right to women's reproductive choice, a just immigration policy, the right to quality and free public education, affordable and de-segregated housing, the right to protect the climate and environment, a government run or single payer health care system, LGBTQ equality, the right of all to vote, the right to peace on the planet.

As hopeful and important as the new developments in movement building are, they do not signal a revolutionary situation. As many of us would like, a cadre party organization with a developed political line is not possible at this time. Such a project can only be undertaken with a far larger and more influential force, one that will guide practical work and develop the strategy for advancement of democracy toward socialist transformation.

Over the years there have been differences on this question in CCDS. At the national convention in 1999 in Raleigh, North Carolina, Charlene Mitchell, then National Co-Chair and National Coordinator, said in her convention opening: "There are some who say we need a revolutionary party...something beyond CofC. They are probably correct. The question is, how is such a party brought into being? Previous experiences show that one cannot successfully declare a party by fiat. The material conditions for the development of a revolutionary party must be in place. The working class must be on the offensive. There must be a growing unity between the potentially revolutionary forces of society."

Over the years, there have been important differences over whether CCDS should even adopt a national organizing priority. It was argued that a national focus would identify the organization within the mass movement and offer a way to sum up practice. At the 1999 convention, this issue was debated intensely and the majority defeated a proposal to help build living wage campaigns as a primary, though not singular, focus for CCDS.

Section 2: Left Unity Efforts from 2009

The consolidation and growth of the Progressive Majority requires the unity of socialists who are oriented towards the mass movements of labor, African Americans, Latinos, Native Americans, Asian Americans, women and youth, and others. Left unity is essential in providing political muscle, organizational consistency, and a vision of a transforming future that are essential for the viability of the Progressive Majority.

One example is the Bernie Sanders campaign which has the potential for advancing a post-electoral Progressive Majority. There is an immediate need for the left to influence the Sanders campaign on the centrality of the anti-racist struggle and for a peaceful foreign policy.

Discussions of left unity took on new urgency at the 2009 CCDS convention in a day-long symposium on left unity and the progressive majority. Participating with CCDS were the Communist Party USA (CPUSA), Democratic Socialists of America (DSA), Solidarity, Freedom Road Socialist Organization (FRSO), and POWER, the precursor to Left Roots. There was a consensus reached that the focus of left unity should be to seek common work in the mass movement to help build the progressive movement.

In March 2013, Mark Solomon, CCDS Co-Chair Emeritus, wrote an article published on Portside, "Whither the Socialist Left? Thinking the 'Unthinkable'". He argued that "The time has come to work for the convergence of socialist organizations committed to non-sectarian democratic struggle, engagement with mass movements, and open debate in search of effective responses to the present crises and to projecting a socialist future."

The following June of 2013, a forum was held in New York City at Service Employees International Union Local 1199, hosted by the Left Labor Project, with CCDS, the CPUSA, DSA, FRSO and the Jacobin Magazine. Speaking for CCDS, Mark Solomon said:

"The quest for left-socialist unity is mandated by the maturing structural crisis of capitalism - with the gap between wealth and the rest of society widening to unprecedented levels. A resulting intensified class war, including an historic assault on labor unions, is driven in significant measure by a vicious right wing that is tearing at the fabric of social payments built up over 75 years."

Solomon concluded with a proposal for "...resolute steps at all levels to form unity committees as soon as possible, to forge united, concrete responses to austerity, to militarization and war, to ecological crisis and to launch the challenging process of building a socialist vision and consciousness. We cannot continue to drift with small, weak organizations resistant to change....The present political and organizational status of the socialist left if unacceptable."

For the most party, Solomon's proposal was not embraced by other organizations represented on the panel. In February 2015, an 8-point program for left unity signed by Carl Davidson, Bill Fletcher and Pat Fry was circulated widely with some positive response from individuals but no organizational traction.

The only concrete response since the 2013 forum has been the development initiated by CCDS in Boston launching the Socialist Unity Project bringing together members of CCDS, CPUSA, DSA, Solidarity, Jacobin study circles and independent progressives. Educational projects and a plan for deciding a common practical initiative in the mass movement are under discussion.

Section 3: Role of the Left

The role of the left is to deepen, concretize and unite the progressive majority with a probing analysis of the system. This will require sound education and mobilization around the continuing threat from the right. There are three immediate tasks:

1) Explain and advance the centrality of the struggle against white supremacy and against the increasingly oppressive and murderous role of police and military - explaining why at this critical juncture in the development of global monopoly capital, systemic violence against people of color is growing and must be defeated;

2) Join with other left forces to build the broadest multiracial electoral coalition along the lines of the Moral Monday movement to pressure the Democratic Party nominee for President whoever it will be. The movement to elect Bernie Sanders should continue to capitalize on the efforts leading up to the Democratic Party convention through organizing at workplaces and neighborhoods, whether or not he will be the nominee. There are opportunities in state and local campaigns as well to promote a progressive agenda, utilizing the electoral arena as an important organizing tool.

3) Play a role in breaking down the fragmentation of the mass movement, advancing and linking together the Fight for $15, union organiz-

ing, immigrant rights, climate justice, anti-war, women's reproductive choice, Black Lives Matter, youth student debt, etc.

Frankly stated, the tasks outstrip our capacity within CCDS as we face a declining membership in numbers and demographics, faltering finances, and weak local chapters. Given this, we should discuss some reorganization to pare down the size of the NCC and NEC and National Co-Chairs. A leaner organizational structure would enable us to better focus energies on left unity initiatives and strengthen our educational work.

The educational resources of our organization should be maintained and strengthened: *Dialogue & Initiative*, *CCDSLinks*, the Online University of the Left, the Carl Bloice Institute for Socialist Education, the Socialist Education Project's monthly discussions, the CC-DS.org web site, the Mobilizer and political statements of CCDS are valuable educational and outreach tools.

This is a period of both crisis and opportunity. The crises of austerity, interventionism, deepening climate crisis, persistent attacks upon Black lives, women's reproductive rights, the right to education and health care, to name a few - are spawning growing resistance of an increasingly coherent and determined progressive majority. We need to meet the challenge inherent in that crisis and attendant opportunity to fight back with confidence in our efforts to contribute to the building of the progressive majority and illuminating the road to a socialist future.

A Program and an Organizing Plan: Keys to Building CCDS and the Left

By Paul Krehbiel

The Committees of Correspondence for Democracy and Socialism
(CCDS) has been discussing our organizational future for the past 8
months in preparation for our 8th
National Convention in Emeryville,
CA, July 29-31, 2016.

After 25 years of excellent work in
the mass movements and in promoting socialism, CCDS membership has declined in recent years.
One reason is that the majority of
our members are from the long
1960's generation of radicals and
are aging, and while some recruitment of new members has taken
place, it has not been enough to reverse the losses. A number of CCDS
leaders and members urge that a change in direction is needed. I agree.
CCDS is not the only socialist organization to experience these problems
- most have. While we need to do a deeper study of why this has happened, we can take steps to reverse this trend now.

First, we are in a new, more favorable political climate, with the political
impact of the recent Occupy Wall Street movement, the Black Lives Matter movement, the climate justice movement, the fight for $15, and the
Bernie Sanders campaign for president, to name just a few. Changing
objective conditions can make a difference

What CCDS needs is to develop a brief, compelling and popular political program, and an organizing plan to rebuild our CCDS membership. This will increase our contribution toward building the broader
left.

Several pre-convention papers urge us to focus on working with the young radicals in socialist groups emerging across the country led by the millennial generation, and focusing our attention on socialist education. I agree with these proposals. But I believe we need to add an organizing component. I believe we should continue to organize in the mass movements, bring activists closer to us, and with the right program and approach, we can recruit new members to CCDS. Even a relatively small number of new members would help us better carry out whatever program our 8th national convention decides upon. To increase the recruitment new CCDS members we need three things: a good program, a good organizing plan, and commitment from at least a core of members to help develop and carry out this program.

If we don't recruit new members our political goals will be harder to realize, and eventually will go unfulfilled as our aging CCDS membership becomes less and less politically active. An organizing plan should be geared especially to young people, and develop a step-by-step plan to work with youth organizations and movements. This plan should have both strong educational and action components. People who are becoming politicized want not only to learn but to act. This seemingly large undertaking is doable by breaking down this organizing project into smaller manageable parts.

There are many historical examples of socialist organizations recruiting young people, or workers, or people of color, and growing in size. Sometimes a large group will join together. Others times one or two will join, then they will convince their peers to join.

During the 1950's Cold War, the left was badly damaged in our country and membership in left organizations shrunk dramatically. The largest Marxist organization, the Communist Party (CP), was still underground well into the 1960's in many locations around the country. In Buffalo, where I grew up and became politically active in the student New Left in my early 20's, the desire to find an organization that had a well thought-out and compelling program for building a movement and winning socialism led some of us to search for something that fit that bill.

The Communist Party had been decimated in Buffalo, and the remaining CP organization there consisted mostly of older members who were still "underground," and not known to the public or us. A slightly "older" leader of the CP came to Buffalo from New York City to set up a CP book table in the student union at the State University at Buffalo during our student strike there in the spring of 1970. The CP leader was African American and most of the student strikers were white, reflecting the student demographics. Several young radical students went to the table to argue with the CP leader. After several conversations, an increasing number of their criticisms and questions were answered, and two of the students were won over to the CP and joined. They then talked to many of their radical student friends and within two years 25 young people joined the CP or its youth organization, the Young Workers Liberation League. I was one of those, joining both organizations.

What convinced us? Learning about an organization that had a compelling, well thought-out program, strategy, and history to build the left, and ultimately socialism, and hearing it from our peers and friends who we trusted. Another attraction was that the CP had committed to helping build a youth organization that we would run ourselves, based on a political program that we had input in developing.

The CP's Method of Recruitment

In the early 1980's I was living and working in Colorado and was active in the Communist Party there. The national CP launched a membership recruiting drive, and laid out a series of steps, which we followed. Recruiting was seen as a process unfolding over a defined period of time. Here are the steps:

1. Each of us made a list of people we knew who we thought might be interested in the CP. Included on that list were people who had demonstrated leadership in their work, and worked in a collective, respectful way that would fit with our style of work. We did not require that each person meet all the criteria we valued. We knew that people grew.

2. We discussed each person on the list in our party club and determined who or what combination of people should talk to each person, and what the approach should be for each person.

3. We worked with the individuals on our list in mass organizations so we could get to know each other better, and observe each other's work.

4. We gave those people who we thought would be interested copies of literature to read, and upon a favorable response, suggested that they might want to subscribe to the party newspaper. We offered short-term gift subscriptions to low income folks who were interested, and to people not quite sure but moving toward us.

5. We set up a Marxist study group and invited people who were close to us to attend. There, we presented the basics of Marxism, the general strategy of the Communist movement and Party program and history, and party life.

6. We asked them to join.

The result was that we increased our membership and political effectiveness considerably. While these methods came from the Communist Party, we can learn something from them. We need to develop our own organizing plan for CCDS, based on our history, beliefs, style of work, and the people we seek to recruit.

Every generation comes to socialism in their own way, and we must respect that. We must encourage them to learn on their own from their own experiences, experiment with various ideas and approaches to politics, make their own mistakes, and draw their own lessons. This is a hallmark of CCDS, features that we embraced at our founding.

Many young people are searching today for a way to get more from their work. Many recognize that being a part of a group that is working together with others to achieve a program that they all agree with, and in an organized, well thought out way, will help build the movement. Yet, they don't want to be in a rigid organization, that is organized from the top down, that restricts their freedom to think, study, explore, experiment, and test various approaches in the real world. CCDS feels the same way. People will join CCDS when they feel they will get something important from being a CCDS member, that it will help them in their work, and to advance the struggle on the issues and vision of a just society that they hold dear.

What follows are some notes that I developed to move toward creating a program and organizing plan. I presented them during the pre-convention discussion. As I wrote then, these are initial ideas, inviting further discussion, debate and change, not words cast in concrete. It is a start. Something to work from, to be amended, or even put aside in favor of a different approach. I welcome all ideas. The goal is how to recruit new members to CCDS.

Pat Fry has presented a very good document to begin our pre-convention discussion. Titled, "The Progressive Majority, Left Unity, and the Tasks of CCDS," she begins by explaining how and why CCDS was founded, the development of the theory of the Progressive Majority as our basic organizing strategy (and proposals to change that strategy), efforts to build left unity, and the role of the left — especially CCDS. I agree with the general framework of our main political document and Pat's presentation.

I want to add to Pat's last paragraph. She states that "the tasks outstrip our capacity within CCDS as we face a declining membership in numbers and demographics, faltering finances, and weak local chapters." Pat recommends that we consider reorganizing the internal structure of CCDS, and focus on left unity and educational work.

I would like to add an organizing component to this, with a detailed and focused organizing plan and strategy to address how to best organize on the ground. Regarding the size of our membership, we have what we have and have to start here. I'm not so concerned by our membership numbers, nor the age of our members. Every revolutionary socialist organization has had both young and older members and leaders. More important is developing the best possible organizing plan and strategy. That can be done with a relatively small number of people. If such a plan is done properly, we will gain new members.

This is not a simple task. A number of efforts have been made to do this and I want to acknowledge and pay tribute to those efforts. Every effort has helped, and has added to our store of knowledge of how to develop an effective organizing strategy. Because this task is difficult, I want to recommend that we make a concerted effort to probe this topic during our pre-convention discussion period, at the convention, and beyond. In my view, this is the most important task before us, precisely because of Pat's assessment of CCDS in her last paragraph. My goal is to begin the discussion of how we can recruit more members, build active and strong chapters, and improve our finances. In short, it requires a detailed organizing plan, with steps, deadlines, and goals.

CCDS has played and continues to play an important and unique role within the left and progressive movements. To see CCDS decline and possibly cease to exist would be a significant loss to the left, the people's movement, and to the larger society. I say this not to slight other left organizations and movements. Almost every organization on the left has a positive role to play. We recognize and welcome the contributions they make. Trying different strategies and tactics, and having different focuses of work, all add to the cumulative knowledge of the left and society and how to conduct our work. Life will reveal which strategies succeed and which need retooling.

When I urge a focus on building CCDS, that does not mean a shift away from mass work, nor theoretical and educational work. To the contrary, mass work, based on rich theoretical and educational work, must be at the center of what we do. The question is: how do we carry out mass work in a way that will best strengthen the mass movements, the broad left, and CCDS.

To begin this discussion, I want to offer several ideas. I am not presenting a fully developed organizing plan. But I'm hopeful that these ideas will stimulate a discussion that will lead to that goal. We need a simple, clear and bold statement of who we are, what we believe, what we want, and how we propose to succeed. This should be printed in many copies for public consumption, posted on-line, and used in our yet to be developed organizing plan. It should be short enough that it can be read in a couple of minutes, and be easily understood by all. This would be the main introduction of CCDS to the people and to those we want to recruit. This would spell out simply what we believe and make it easy for people to say, "Yes, I agree with that, and I know why I'm joining." What follows is a first draft of that proposed document; I welcome feedback, discussion, amendments, etc.

Draft Statements

Committees of Correspondence for Democracy and Socialism (CCDS): Who We Are

CCDS is an organization of people of all races, nationalities and ages, women and men, who work to improve life for the vast majority of people. We seek to empower people by expanding democracy in all areas of life, building and strengthening the working-class, people of color and women, and progressive movements and organizations working on all issues that impact people's lives.

We want to find common ground to unite people and organizations, and work toward building a society free from exploitation and oppression, where every person can live fulfilling and happy lives — a society we call socialism. We believe that building a larger, stronger and more effective CCDS will help achieve these goals.

What We Believe

We believe the major impediment to happy and fulfilling lives for millions of people is the inordinate power of large corporations and financial institutions inherent in the capitalist system to affect our economic, political, and social lives, for better or worse. This capitalist elite uses their power to enrich themselves at the expense of their workers, and everyone else. We believe that the dominate power of this capitalist class must be broken up in order to free people to pursue their goals and dreams within the context of a society committed to fairness, justice, equality and the well being of everyone, socialism.

What We Want

We have an immediate 12-point program, and a long-term program. Working to achieve our 12 point program will lay the foundation to achieve our long-term program.

12 Point program

1. We want full employment for all those seeking to work.

2. We want jobs that pay enough to ensure a safe, secure and comfortable life for everyone. Today, we believe that a $20 minimum wage is needed.

3. We want to end all predatory pricing of goods and services by enacting an excess profits tax and other measures in order to keep prices, especially for the necessities of life, affordable for everyone, including small businesses.

4. We want everyone who seeks to form or join a union, or to exercise their union rights, to be able to do so without interference from employers or any other entity, and with full support from the government and legal system.

5. We want a society free from racism, sexism, and all forms of discrimination, using affirmative action programs to achieve this goal, and enforceable laws with penalties to help safeguard these protections.

6. We want high quality health care provided to all, an improved Medicare for All single-payer system, regardless of ability to pay, funded by progressive taxation.

7. We want free college for all and the protection of our public school system. We want a meaningful education from pre-school through university, with courses that reflect the needs and interests of our diverse multi-racial, multi-national people.

8. We want medical and family leave extended to all, and especially a new mother and father who should have 6 months of paid family leave to take care of their baby. Develop a free system of day care centers.

9. We want a foreign policy that builds solidarity between the people of the US and other countries, based on peace, mutual respect, and cooperation. This will require cutting the massive military budget and shifting money to social needs.

10. We want tax reform where the very wealthy and large corporations pay their fair share to ensure the financing of all social programs. This will require raising their taxes, but not the taxes of the bottom 90% of society. Close all tax loopholes for the wealthy and corporations.

11. Expand democratic rights and practices in all areas and institutions of society, and reverse all laws that give corporations and the wealthy extra power, such as Citizens United.

12. Weaken the power of capitalism, especially the power of the elite capitalists, and replace that dynamic of exploitation and oppression of others with relationships that facilitate sharing, cooperation, nurturing and ensuring the well-being of all, in short with the building blocks of socialism.

Our long term program is to consolidate the victories achieved on our 12 point program, expand those victories so they become the central fabric of life and embodied in our laws and popular culture, while establishing legal structures to protect and advance progress on the road to creating a fully developed socialist society. (We should add something here to describe the general features of a socialist society, recognizing that is built in steps as part of an on-going process.)

How We Will Achieve These Goals

We will achieve these goals by building and supporting organizations and political and social movements that are working for these goals, with the working-class, people of color, and women playing a leadership role.

We recognize that all effective political movements need leadership to succeed. We seek to help develop leaders and a leadership structure that is chosen democratically by the members and people involved, that comes from the bottom up and is elected by the people, is accountable to the people, is reflective of the diversity of our people, and can be removed by a democratic decision. Organizations and leaders exist to work toward achieving goals, not to ensure the perpetuation of any leader or organization. There are models of organization that fulfill these requirements. In a work setting, a fully democratic union Stewards Council is one example. (I'll comment on this briefly later.)

We also recognize that we must build CCDS by recruiting more members and by increasing our effectiveness.

In order to recruit more members we have to be involved in mass movements and organizations, identify the politically advanced left people in these movements, and develop a comprehensive recruitment plan. Such a plan must have an educational component comprised of well organized classes, conducted in many locations around the country. While we want to recruit from all sectors of society, we should focus special attention on the working-class, people of color, women, and young millennials who are already politically active or who are searching for solutions to the problems we face today. Our chief goal should be to build a youth organizing committee with the goal of forming a youth organization, which will be led and run by the youth, and affiliated to CCDS.

This will require a well thought Organizing Plan. This plan will address in detail organizing in mass movements, and organizing among leftists, and developing education and political work for both. This plan must have at its center a specific plan to recruit new members into CCDS.

Developing a good Organizing Plan is key to building CCDS. A good Organizing Plan has a number of component parts. I want to mention just two briefly here in the hope that it will generate further discussion. When I talk about organizing, I'm not so much talking about the skills needed to run a meeting, locate the proper venue, do outreach and other similar tasks. All of those are vitally important. I want to focus here instead on the components of a political Organizing Plan.

There are two basic components: (1) having well thought-out long-term political goals, and (2) the specific methods and steps to achieve them. CCDS has done a lot of good work discussing #1, formulating political goals. CCDS members also have a rich history working in mass movements, using a variety of methods (strategies and tactics) to build them and make them more effective. But we have not done a systematic study of what strategies and tactics worked best and under what specific circumstances, what our short and long term goals are, what methods will likely be the most effective in achieving them, and developing plans to guide us in the achievement of our goals.

Some short and long-term goals may overlap in time, but generally short term goals are specific goals that we can work on today, while long-term goals generally require successful completion of many short term goals first. It usually helps to establish the long-term goals first, even if just in a general form, and then work backward, establishing the steps that must be taken to move us from where we are toward the longer-term goals. It is essential to have a leader(s) or chief organizer(s) who has a general idea of both short and long-term goals and how they inter-relate, and who is respected by their peers and/or co-workers.

Here is an example of how this works. In the trade union movement we may set a series of long-term goals to make the unions more class consciousness, more politically left, more effective in defending current gains, winning new improvements, playing a leadership role in social justice campaigns, and in building a progressive independent electoral strategy to elect progressives and socialists to political office and defeat reactionary ones.

What short-term, realizable steps can be taken to help workers reach these long-term bigger goals? One short-term goal to help this process is to organize democratic, member-run Stewards Councils at the work-place. When organized properly, these Stewards Councils empower the workers, educating them about their rights and how to protect them, teaching them how to set higher more advanced goals, teaching them through experience how to work together for a common goal, and how to take the members through a work-site campaign so they can experience what empowerment feels like.

Most people learn best when education is combined with activity that they participate in directly. Setting simple activities that they can easily participate in, like handing out leaflets to co -workers, or getting co-workers to sign a petition, as one part of a larger strategy, will help advance that worker's personal development. It's also important to set short term goals that can be won so they see that their efforts made a difference. All of these small realizable steps and experiences, when linked to a larger strategy and specific goals, turn an unorganized and undirected group of individual workers into an organized and directed collective. That is an important prerequisite in building the strength needed to win the next set of larger goals. And it forms a building block in their consciousness to internalize the advantages of cooperation. This also becomes a building block of socialism.

We should focus considerable attention on the younger generations, helping them advance their own projects and organizations as they see fit, but also recruiting into CCDS those who are close to us politically. We should also be available to help them develop as leaders, but recognize that leadership should be earned. While most left, revolutionary and socialist movements and revolutions have young people in leading positions, the overall leadership was and is composed of people of all ages.

Paul Krehbiel is a long time union organizer. He has also been involved in organizing political, community, and social justice campaigns, and is a member of the National Coordinating Committee of CCDS.

Comments: *Pat Fry said,*

Thanks to Paul for his contribution on a plan for organizing to build the mass movement and CCDS. I think working to build chapters at the local level is the main task of the organization if it is going to grow. We cannot remain as we are now.

One question that I want to provocatively pose to further this discussion is the following: at this political moment, what is CCDS' unique role and is it sufficient to mandate building an organization apart from other socialist organizations that play a non-sectarian role in the mass movement?

Duncan McFarland said,

Hello Paul. Yes, thank you. CCDS needs a systematic organizing plan to build and promote itself. You say, "CCDS has played and continues to play an important and unique role within the left and progressive movements." Can you spell out concretely in more detail what that role is? Articulating a persuasive answer to this question is pretty much the raison d'etre of CCDS and the central message for recruiting new members.

You suggest a written description of what CCDS is about that takes two minutes to read. In addition, how about a 20 second elevator speech? E.g. "CCDS works for left unity, has an outstanding socialist education program and the XYZ campaign in the mass movements." We need a more focused and prioritized program on the national level of the organization.

Paul Krehbiel responds:

First, there are many areas of general agreement among socialist organizations which we recognize and applaud. When I say CCDS is "unique" I do not mean superior. Some differences among socialist organizations create a diversity that is healthy. CCDS is a pluralist socialist organization which encourages grassroots initiatives and tries various approaches to see what works best. We welcome that diversity within CCDS and the broader left, and believe it is a strength. Many of the differences aren't substantive, but rather a difference of degree. CCDS's emphasis on certain issues and organizing approaches may be a little different than other left organizations.

For example, the emphasis we place on race, gender and class keeps us focused on the centrality of the fight against racism and white supremacy, and male supremacy, and the interconnection of these struggles with our efforts to strengthen the working class and its organized expression in the trade unions and the broader labor movement. Our goal should be to unite the broadest political forces possible while finding ways to help move large circles of people to more advanced left positions. CCDS has been an early and consistent advocate of left unity based on common areas of agreement, even if just one or two initially. I see building

left unity as a step-by-step process. We seek to find common ground and work together on those points of agreement. CCDS combines the best of the 2nd Socialist International (democracy and grassroots initiative, for example), and the 3rd Communist International (striving to

develop a solid Marxist analysis of social forces, a focused plan of work, and well thought-out strategy to win based on the working class and its allies, for example), and every other theoretical and practical work and practice that aids the advancement of humanity (our work to build and strengthen the Progressive Majority and 21st Century socialism).

I think building and strengthening CCDS does not conflict with building left unity and a stronger left and, in fact, will help this process. In addition to a brief but bold program, CCDS should also have a short "elevator" speech, though there is no substitute for developing deep, working relationships with others to advance all political work.

CCDS Future Directions: A Consolidated Program of Political Analysis and Socialist Education, Rooted in Mass Struggle: For Pre-Convention Discussion

By Duncan McFarland

Consider both the world situation and needs of the larger left movement in the US. Globally, climate change is growing worse, and while there was political progress at COP21 in Paris, measures to respond are still inadequate. Countries are modernizing their nuclear arsenals and wars are constant. In the US, the rich get richer while others struggle, racism and anti-immigrant sentiment is increasing. On the other hand, leftist social movements are strengthening, the prestige of socialism is increasing among young people, and there is rising populist energy on both the left and right. Confidence in mainstream institutions has fallen to a low point; this polarization is reflected in the enthusiasm for Sanders and Trump in the presidential campaign.

In the world today, US capitalism/imperialism is losing economic clout, has ceded all moral authority, and has declining political influence. US policy more and more relies on its only trump card, military power. Is this the period of the final decline of global capitalism? It is difficult to predict whether capitalism will again renew itself as it has always done since the many crises of the post-World War I era, but certainly this is a time of weakening of the system and an opportunity for a strong anti-capitalist movement.

Marx and Engels clearly foresaw in general terms the eventual breakdown of capitalism, leading to revolution and socialism. They described in scientific terms the historic role of the communists, socialists and working class as the leading force in the transformation to the new society. Setting aside for now consideration of the role of the five states internationally, which are a product of socialist revolution (Cuba, China, Vietnam, Laos and North Korea), the socialist movement in the US is today fragmented, lacks power and is mostly ineffective in stepping up to fulfill its historic mission. This poses a dilemma, there are "no shortcuts" in rebuilding socialism yet the time of day requires urgency. Much that is relevant can be learned from left movements especially in Latin America and Europe.

How does CCDS fit into this picture? As historical materialists, we should look to its 20+ years of organizational experience. The original vision was of a socialist organization that would preserve the best politics of the Communist Party in a new organizational form emphasizing democratic process and grassroots participation. Other socialist perspectives would be welcome to enrich the dialogue and attract the many unaffiliated individuals. A vibrant organizing center would grow and make a substantial contribution to the eventual formation of a broader formation with a large working class and people of color membership. Class struggle was recognized as the driving force and leadership would have strong representation by workers of color and immigrant workers, women, and those of non-traditional sexuality.

Eventually, CCDS would combine with other forces and transition into something bigger and stronger, perhaps a working class political party. Unfortunately, the coalescence and expansion of the democratic socialist movement has not yet happened.

Along the way, however, CCDS has developed expertise and accomplished a lot in political analysis and socialist education: the many discussions and presentations online, at conferences and in person; insightful political positions on current issues; Dialogue and Initiative; various pamphlets; Portside as a spinoff; the Online University of the Left; and, the annual youth schools. Its richness comes from the rooting of theory in the act of mass struggle. If these separate parts were connected into one program, it would be outstanding in its breadth and quality.

Experience shows that socialist collaboration is easier to achieve when working together on an educational project, with unity in mass work the next and more difficult step. A CCDS initiated program of 21st century socialist education could be a substantive contribution to facilitating cooperation and strengthening the left.

Meanwhile, the time has passed for the 1960s activist generation to form the leadership core for social transformation or revolution in the US. Older folks have a seat at the table, an important voice in decisions and may still make a critical contribution. However, the still challenging decisions on structure and action program for the socialist movement will mostly be made by younger comrades.

As a member of the Boston Jacobin reading group and as a Left Roots compa, I have been impressed by the commitment of younger social-ists and radicals to read, study and learn in their drive to create 21st century socialism. But there are inevitable limitations: lack of in-depth focus on Marxism and scientific socialism; a one-sided perspective on the achievements of the Soviet Union, China and 20th century socialism; and, minimal knowledge of communist and labor history in the US.

CCDS has strengths in those very areas where the younger comrades could use support. In addition, we bring understanding of the centrality of racism, as well as class and gender, and the ability to underscore the importance of the democratic movements and building the progressive majority. CCDS has contributions to make in left strategy and unity, and skills learned in the long course of struggle.

Consequently, CCDS can play a role connecting existing activities into a consolidated program to be expanded and developed, a program of socialist discussion, analysis and education. This must flow from and inform participation in mass struggles. Popular education tools can be created. This can be a signature program of the organization, with spe-cial efforts to connect with the Next Left and the emerging socialist youth movement. This program would recognize and build upon the strengths of CCDS and open a path for growth.

Duncan McFarland is the chair of the Peace and Solidarity Committee of CCDS and a member of the CCDS National Coordinating Committee.

Harry Targ said,

My prior post concentrated on mass work with special attention directed at elections and building a progressive majority. Helping to Build a Pro-gressive Majority has been a major CCDS project since our Living Wage Campaign of the 1990s, the development of the Socialist Education Proj-ect at the dawn of the new century and our documents about Building the Progressive Majority around the 2004-2005 period. I think CCDS can continue to play a role in this work as the blog essay argues.

Having said that I applaud the Socialist thrust and the youth focus of the excellent statements by Carl and Duncan. I also endorse the continua-tion of the vibrant CCDS revolutionary education component they refer to. My only reservations about the two statements are the following:

1.While youth have always played an instrumental role in movements for social change, I remain uncomfortable privileging age as the critical variable around which left politics should revolve. Such an approach can encourage younger comrades to dismiss history, older activists, and older political traditions. In addition, on occasions, such highlighting of youth can lead to what I see as pandering. Most importantly, as with the organic connections we make theoretically between issues involving class, race, and gender; war and the environment; inequality and loss of democracy; we should also project the vision of the connections between the past, the present, and the future. History matters. The present matters. And both relate to a better future.

2.While CCDS needs to be realistic, assess its weaknesses as well as its strengths, I think it is counter-productive to project an image of an organization in decline, or transition. We should commit ourselves to change and adaptation to new material conditions. Our flexibility since 1992 has been one of its most interesting features.

CarlDavidson said,

That every revolution is history has been mainly made up of fighters from the age of 18 to 40 is a demographic fact, and even their leadership was not much older. That is not 'pandering' or 'ageism,' and it doesn't mean that older comrades don't have much to offer or don't have a valuable role. It simply gives us an accurate perspective on how to focus.

Challenging White Supremacy is Critical to Efforts for Transformative Change

By Meta Van Sickle, Carla F Wallace and Janet Tucker

From top: Meta Van Sickle, Carla Wallace, Janet Tucker

There is a battle going on for the hearts, minds, bodies and votes of white people in this country and both direct and indirect appeals to racism are part of an old strategy with new legs.

Trump's message of hate, Islamophobia, racism and division, his calls for outright violence against protestors in his rallies and his strategies of wall-building and deportation are gaining more traction than most people, who care deeply about these issues, ever thought it would. All over the country white people are flocking to hear Trump, lining up for hours in big and small towns around the country to get into his rallies. Many of these people are poor and working class white people. Union leaders are warning that his targeting of white working people is working and the demographic studies of Trump supporters bear them out.

While too many white leftists and too many white progressives hesitate to take on our responsibility for organizing white people for racial justice, corporate America is taking the race based class divisions all the way to the bank and creating a country in which people of color are seen as ever more expendable.

A recent New York Times article documents the demographic breakdown of Trump supporters. The strongest indicator is a white person who

has not finished high school, has no work, and has given up looking for it (Neil and Katz, 2016).

According to liberals, many progressives, and the mainstream media, you would think that we have a phenomena of poor and working class white people as hopeless bigots. You would think that racism was invented by poor and working class white people and that this is who is sustaining systemic racism and white supremacy throughout our country and influencing this country's relationships with other countries.

Over and over we hear, "It's those uneducated rednecks," as we wash our hands of the responsibility to do more than blame from the sidelines as Muslims, Black and Brown people, and immigrants bear the brunt of the dangerous winds of racialized hate blowing across our land.

In his important article, "Donald Trump is Dangerous", *The Nation's* John Nichols points out that Trump is speaking to working class anxiety more effectively and powerfully than mainstream democrats. "This country is dying," says Trump. "And our workers are losing their jobs." Trump goes on to decry trade pacts and threatens to tax corporations if they continue to move jobs out of the country. Nichols quotes AFL-CIO president Richard Trumka, who tells him that his workers are talking to him about Trump, and Service Employees International Union president Mary Kay Henry, who cautions that the Trump message is so on target for white workers that he could win enough union votes, and even the presidency, with an over-all program that will hurt white workers, and all workers.

Instead of addressing the concerns of poor and working families, front and center, Washington talks about the economic "recovery", "revitalized" manufacturing and "progress" on clean energy. Meanwhile, there continues to be urban centers where unemployment runs close to 50 percent among young Black men, and rural poverty, which promises to keep several generations from providing enough for families to get by. What has been left of the safety net is being shredded further everywhere you look. A recent example under the Republican governor of Kentucky, is the choice between canceling Family Court or Drug Court because budget cuts do not allow for keeping both.

There is a reason that the Trump rhetoric resonates and it is not only because it caters to racism and blames people of color. Trump is playing to the deep seated insecurity and material hardships that white working class and low income people are experiencing due to the failure of this economic system. And yes, he is wrapping this in attacks on people of color. His message is racist and it only leads to a working class further divided along racial lines and unable to grow the people power needed for real change that benefits all of us.

This racist agenda and this divided working class is taking a toll on white workers in many ways. A recent study shows that the only demographic whose mortality rate is rising is white workers. The causes of death are disproportionately from alcohol, drug addiction, and suicide. Despite the rhetoric about an economic recovery, and despite the "buffer" of race afforded white workers, working people are facing the direct impact of capitalism in decline and are literally dying from it. While institutional racism ensures that people of color, in particular Black people, bear the brunt of the oppression, white workers as well, have lost the hope that they can provide a better future for their children. Unlike people of color, many of whom, as Audre Lorde wrote, knew they were "never meant to survive," poor and working class whites thought that they were meant to survive.

A snapshot of parts of the South is particularly helpful in this regard. While people of color are bearing the overwhelming impact of the continuing recession, working class people of all colors are facing cutbacks in basic services, loss of jobs, and lowering or stagnant wages. New industries may be moving to South Carolina for example, but their reasons for doing so have nothing to do with improving the economic health of the area. Quite the opposite. These industries are moving there because they are paying little or no state or local taxes and wages far lower than in their sister plants in other locations in the country, according to the Charleston Central Labor Council, Personal Communication. Corporate welfare and low wages limit the public sector's ability to deliver in several ways, from the underfunding and defunding of public education, to the poorly maintained infrastructure, such as roads and bridges, to a lack of access to affordable health care and so on.

If we are to counter the use of bigotry to divert people from the failures of capitalism or to seduce white people falling out of the economy into the lure of having their own strongman, those of us who are white need to step up to our responsibility to do the work with other white people around racial justice. We need to be connecting with other working class and poor white people, our families, our neighbors and our co-workers, who need a system that works for the many, not just the few. In this moment, we must move from blaming and shaming poor and working class white people or, in other words, avoid the urgency of challenging white supremacy, and take up the work of lifting up the mutual interest we have in an America that provides for the basic human needs of all people AND is anchored in an unapologetic commitment to racial justice.

Part of our work must be to shine a light on those examples of white working class people joining with people of color for a mutual interest agenda that benefits all. Robin Kelley's brilliant book, *Hammer and Hoe: Alabama Communists during the Great Depression,* notes stories in the 1930's of cross race, class conscious worker struggles against barriers to voting rights for poor people in rural areas. There are many examples of cross race class solidarity from the coal mines in Appalachia. In July of 1891 over 1,500 miners freed prisoners in the shadow of Tennessee Coal and Iron Company. The Chattanooga Federation of Trades reported that "whites and Negroes are standing shoulder to shoulder" and armed with 840 rifles. Black and white workers joined together in the Paint Creek Cabin strike of 1913-14 and in many battles against King Coal in the decades to follow.

More recently, outside the Louisville Convention Center in Kentucky on March 1, 2016 thousands of white people, many of them working class, lined up to hear Donald Trump deride big government and its elite corporate allies. Promising to "make America great again" his increasingly popular message is wrapped in blaming the nation's woes on immigrants, "freeloaders" and other barely coded language for people of color. But also there, were members of Louisville Showing Up for Racial Justice (SURJ), part of a national network dedicated to organizing white people in effective, accountable relationships with people of color led struggles engaged not only in disrupting the Trump gathering on the inside, but also engaging on the outside. This included connecting with some in the Trump crowd around our mutual interest in an economy that works for all of us and the idea that we can win if white and people of color join together. In one conversation, a white worker at the Trump rally said that he thought one of the problems with so many Black people being put in prison is that so many of the judges are rich and white. In that brief exchange is the possibility of shifting the blame from people of color to the elites on both sides of the political aisle, who have failed to address the growing economic divide between rich and poor and the increasing impoverishment of the US poor and working class. Rather than blaming white workers for their fear and anxiety, SURJ frames racial justice as being in the mutual interest of ALL workers and urges unity across racial lines as the only way to win the jobs, housing, health care, clean environment and dignity we all want and need.

Too often, rural people, many of whom are working class whites, are broad brushed as being the breeding ground of right wing militia. However, the leaders of much of this activity are far better off economically than those they seek to engage. In rural Oregon, over 350 mostly rural people came together outside Burns to say no to the militias holed up in the federal wildlife sanctuary. Supported by efforts of the Rural Organizing Project, the gathering exposed the lie that big city dwellers often have about low income rural white people going along with, or worse, instigating right wing, racist militia mobilizations.

Charleston Area Justice Ministries (CAJM) is an example of the work that is possible when we focus on the stake that both whites and people of color have in racial justice. In work on the intersections between racism, gun violence prevention and police preemptive stop reduction activities, the group has exposed the disproportionate targeting of people of color communities by police. CAJM has researched the number of "pretext" police stops across the police departments in the state. The North Charleston police department made over 130,000 such stops last year. Seventy percent of the stops were of African American drivers though the African American population is only forty two percent.

The CAJM group is now in the process of inviting the two cities' mayors and police chiefs into a conversation about these police procedures in the presence of hundreds of concerned community members. The group is calling for a commitment to reduce the number of pretext stops, an outside auditor to review the stops and better community policing practices. A mutual interest narrative can address the reality of police oppression in Black communities and inspire the development of the changes that will make ALL communities safer.

The central point of right wing populism is white supremacy and the use of racism to blame people of color for the woes of white working people. Linda Alcoff, in her book, *The Future of Whiteness*, explains that white liberals "remain uncomfortable in broaching the topic (of race), while white conservatives generally try to disguise their racial references, though the disguise is often so ineffective as to be a joke" (p. SSS).

Too many efforts among white liberals and some white leftists have either fallen into the mistake of avoiding the issue of race as divisive to class unity or speaking of a "white privilege" few struggling white workers can identify with. The first approach maintains the fertile ground for appeals to racism, the second erases the class differences in how white people of wealth and white workers experience their whiteness. Both continue the strategic errors in our efforts to build working class unity on a basis of shared needs, hopes, and a commitment to racial justice.

Lee Atwater, in his book *Bad Boy*, aptly describes how the right wing politicians are using "wedge" issues to divide and conquer the voting population. One such current wedge is the narrow and inaccurate portrayal of the Democratic Party as being anti-police. While those of us engaged in challenging police abuse see this suggestion as laughable, white voters who have already bought into the idea that police terror in Black communities and the killings of Black people is reasonable and appropriate, are shunning Democratic candidates as anti-police. In North Charleston, SC the police shooting of Walter Scott was greeted by at least three popular responses, some of which were only voiced in cloistered spaces: 1) outrage at the police violence, 2) outrage that there was outrage at the shooting (Scott deserved it and the person who made the video should have been shot too), and 3) indifference.

A mutual interest framework, that focuses on the stake that both working class white people and people of color have in accountable policing, jobs, housing, healthcare and other basic necessities, and the humanity that anchors us to one another can grow the unity to challenge Trumpism, Wall Street, crazy Cruz Republicans, and the divisions that keep us from the transformative changes we all need.

We must be willing to talk about how race is being used to divide working people and who benefits when we are divided. But most importantly, we must move beyond talking about this with one another and take a mutual interest narrative that centers racial justice in the neighborhoods, workplaces and families in which we live, work and love. In particular, white people on the left who are serious about challenging capitalism must heed the call made over a half century ago by our sisters and brothers of color in SNCC, and our comrades in the Black Panther Party, for white people to "organize our own". In the words of SNCC leader Stokely Carmichael, "One of the most disturbing things about almost all the white supporters of the movement has been that they are afraid to go into their own communities–which is where the racism exists-and work to get rid of it." Those of us who are white must learn how to speak about white supremacy and how it is hurting all of us in white communities.

Inspired by the movement for Black lives, Black youth taking to the streets at great risk to challenge police abuse, undocumented Latino youth calling for immigration reform, the largely people of color base of the Fight for $15, and indigenous leadership in the anti-pipeline environmental struggle, more and more white people are asking what they can do about racism. They are struggling to understand what racial justice has to do with their own liberation. This development provides an opening for white progressives and the left to take up our responsibility to organize white people for racial justice as part of an ever growing multiracial movement for transformative change.

This moment is ripe with opportunities to do this work, and burdened with dangers if we do not. One example of a broad based effort organizing white working people for racial justice is the national SURJ network. Moving with a mutual interest framework (that what we all need to live in dignity and have our needs met is bound up in the struggle for racial justice and that appeals to racism only benefit those in power) SURJ has a focus on the critical role of the south and on white working class and poor people, including rural, youth, LGBTQ and disabled people.

Black Lives Matter founder Alicia Garza says that white people need to break white silence, challenge white supremacy and create a pole to which other white people can gravitate. Providing a response to the call from the movement for Black lives to mobilize hundreds of thousands of white people in effective, accountable action with people of color led struggles, chapters of SURJ have organized all over the country (140 and more each month in cities big and small and rural areas). People wanting to set up a SURJ Chapter get help from the national network with resources and organizing training.

If we are to counter the hate and divisive messages that are directed at the fears and real life struggles of white working class and poor people, white progressives and those on the left need to get out of our "comfort zones" and use our voices and bodies to say no to white supremacy. We must organize white people to stand with people of color or communities that work for all of us.

Rather than wringing our hands over what is to be done, Louisville SURJ goes door to door in white working class neighborhoods talking about how police are targeting Black communities and why the divisions between white and Black workers keep all of us from winning the change we need to provide for our families. In a recent afternoon of conversations with over 120 white families, over 60 agreed to put a Black Lives Matter yard sign in their yard.

As white southern civil rights activist Anne Braden told us years ago, "The battle is and always has been a battle for the hearts and minds of white people in this country. The fight against racism is our issue. It's not something that we're called on to help people of color with. We need to become involved with it as if our lives depended on it because really, in truth, they do."

As Alcoff notes, "…pessimism breeds the fatalism that excuses inaction and complicity." Whether it is organizing with SURJ, working with existing campaigns and organizations like the Sanders campaign, working with a local union drive or engaging in other efforts, we can be part of a movement to bring hundreds of thousands of white working people into motion for an agenda that challenges corporate greed, undermines patriarchy, ends war and demands racial justice. Both the today and the tomorrow of every one of us demands no less.

References

Alcoff, Linda. (2015). *The Future of Whiteness*. Malden, MA: Polity Press.

Irwin, Neil and Katz, Josh. (2016, March 12). 'The Geography of Trumpism." *The New York Times: The Upshot*, Retrieved from http://www.nytimes.com/2016/03/13/upshot/the-geography-of-trumpism.html?smprod=nytcore-iphone&smid=nytcore-iphone-share&_r=0

Time of Day: The Politics of Chaos

By Harry Targ

During the twentieth century the dominant circumstances of political life were clear. As capitalism evolved from manufacturing to finance, the character of international relations changed. Crude militarism, while constant, was increasingly aided by covert operations, and most importantly by economic penetration.

The United States as the hegemonic actor on the world stage during most of the century was the clear target of anti-war activism and class struggle at home. National liberation movements rose up to resist the drive for imperial control. Since contradictions existed in international and intranational affairs our task was clearly to struggle against imperialism, monopoly capitalism, racism and sexism.

Twenty-first century global political economy is also characterized by these key features. Perhaps the "grand narrative," as post-modernists would call it, remains the same. But, and this is critical, the politics of daily life is far more complicated and it is these complications that give the appearance of chaos. The old narrative and the chaos we experience need to be understood together; particularly among those of us who are committed to the vision of a twenty-first century socialism.

First, the current violence in the Middle East/Persian Gulf is escalating and spreading to other regions. The vicious violence in Paris and Beirut by presumably ISIS followers leads to mass murder. ISIS seems to represent a new brutal form of anti-systemic violence that shows no mercy or humanity. It has its roots in French and British colonial rule in the Middle East, United States collaboration with the Saudi monarchy, western support for the creation of the state of Israel in contradiction to those living on the land, a US-led war on Iraq in 1991, and the US wars of the twenty-first century in Afghanistan and Iraq. Blood is on the hands of every western power in the region but, in terms of victims of violence everywhere, blood also is on the hands of ISIS, Al Qaeda, the Syrian government, Saudi Arabia and the Emirates, Russia, and Iran. Violence is about economic control, political hegemony, nationalism, resistance, and, perhaps to a lesser extent, religious sectarianism and fundamentalisms. The violence is also about arms transfers, racism, and hate.

Second, imperial violence proceeds as global capitalism consolidates its control of the economies of the world. The Transpacific Partnership creates a so-called free trade zone covering about forty percent of the globe and is in the process prefiguring a challenge to Chinese influence in Asia. To complete the "Asian pivot" the United States has increased its military presence in the South China Sea by further cooperating militarily with the Philippines and Japan.

Third, very much below the radar, the United States expands its military presence in Africa with the establishment of AFRICOM, arms aid, and training of militaries on the continent. Presumably, the US militarization of Africa would check the growing economic influence of China.

Fourth, international and domestic violence, economic decay, and threats to life itself, are inextricably connected to the rapidly deteriorating global climate brought on by fossil fuels. Devastating changes in climate-flooding, draught, rising sea levels, life-threatening hurricanes, tsunamis, earthquakes-make life more unbearable and are coupled with economic inequality, the global distribution of weapons, and rising ethnic animosities leading to hopelessness, violence, and rightwing populist anger.

Within the United States the attack on workers, Blacks, and women escalates to an almost fever pitch. Households living below livable wages reach 35-40 percent in many states. Real wages and steady jobs with benefits decline. Economic circumstances among African Americans and Latinos lag behind whites by 10 to 30 percent. And the inequality in the distribution of the wealth of US society increases.

Attacks on Blacks increase in the streets, in the political arena, in public schools and in higher education. Black Lives Matter, the Fight for Fifteen, and recent protests on over 100 college campuses reflect fightbacks against the escalation of systemic assaults on people of color. And we cannot forget that a prime mover of the toxic atmosphere of American political life is fueled by profound racial hatred of a president who happens to be an African American.

The assault upon women, particularly vile campaigns to shut down Planned Parenthood, and brazen homophobia reflected in so-called religious freedom campaigns spread throughout the nation.

And the real meanings, the master narrative about war, violence, exploitation, racism, and sexism are masked by a media discourse that transforms politics from concrete realities to the partial truths about terrorism, the threats to free speech, arguments about political correctness, and the need to be tough, vigilant, and armed to protect the so-called national security of the United States at home and abroad. Media frames fuel and are fueled by a growing rightwing populism in the United States and Europe that ironically mirrors the rise of terrorism in the Middle East, Asia, and Africa.

As we reflect upon the movement-building of the twentieth century and the context of a seeming "politics of chaos" in the twenty-first century, the tasks of the Left are clear. First, it needs to clarify, refine, and develop the "grand narrative" about the global political economy and its connections with capital accumulation, class, race, gender, homophobia, and the environment. The theory and practices of the twentieth century were not wrong. But they need to be adapted to the seeming economic, political, and environmental chaos of today.

Second, the left needs also to do what it has always done: fightback against all reaction, international and domestic. Today this includes resisting expanding war and imperialism abroad and challenging racism, chauvinism, police violence, and the destruction of existing government programs at home. And this fightback has been increasing on a worldwide basis.

Professor Harry Targ, based in West Lafayette, Indiana, is active in the peace and justice movements in the midwest rural agricultural heartland of America.

21st Century Revolutionary Education: A Discussion Document Socialist Education Project (SEP), Committees of Correspondence for Democracy and Socialism (CCDS)

By Janet Tucker, Meta Van Sickle, Duncan McFarland, Harry Targ and Carl Davidson

As the twenty-first century un-folds we need to examine our approach to revolutionary edu-cation and the role of the SEP. Almost a decade ago, the Com-mittees of Correspondence for Democracy and Socialism (CCDS) proposed that the organization devel-op a Socialist Education Project (SEP). The proposal came at a time when the promise of the "new economy," built on the growth of the Silicon Valley, had begun to fade.

Neo-liberal globalization, so much celebrated by every United States administration since the late 1970s, continued to generate inequalities in wealth and income all around the globe. The process of financial-ization, a systemic economic shift from the production of goods and services to financial speculation, undergirded the growing pathology of capitalist development. In this economic and political environment, mainstream commentators began to write about the insights that Marx and his followers brought to the study of capitalism. So it seemed to us in CCDS that a socialist political organization needed to explore rigorous study of the evolution of capitalism, Marxist analysis of how it works, and the logical possibilities for alternatives to it, particularly socialist ones.

The SEP was created. Local CCDS activists launched study groups. Members of the SEP committee generated reading materials to support local study groups. Some materials were assembled as "modules," or integrated short courses with readings, questions for study, and bibliographic suggestions. These modules are still available for use.

Over the past several years the SEP has hosted a number of national discussions. We have discussed both books and current events and articles of current interest. However, most discussions have been topical around current issues more than theoretical events. In addition, over the past year we have held "4th Monday" of the month teleconference discussions on a multitude of subjects. These discussions among 10-15 teleconference participants, while excellent, have not engaged the vast majority of our membership.

On Socialist Pedagogy

We want to address the question of pedagogy, specifically the process of learning. We believe that there is a socialist practice that is relevant to our education and our political activities and they are connected. In other words, when we form study groups they should be socialist study groups. These connections are well described in our book, 'The Struggle for a Substantive Democracy.' The book is designed with young activists' study groups as the primary audience.

People learn political principles through practice as well as through theory. One of the most influential educational theorists, from the vantage point of radical socialist change, was Brazilian educator Paulo Friere. His book, The Pedagogy of the Oppressed, influenced revolutionaries and reformers around the world, particularly at the grassroots level in the Global South. We have discussed Friere, but we need to continue our discussion, adding insights from other theorists such as Gramsci, Vygotsky, Piaget and contemporaries such as Henry Giroux. For example, Heather Clayton explored five main points embedded in Freire's work. According to her, Paulo Friere emphasized:

1. The importance of dialogue and the fact that the dialogue was bidirectional and contained within the bounds of a respectful relationship. It meant that all participants in an educational setting must work together. In political groups, discussions should involve equally intellectual individuals, those who primarily teach and write, and community activists;

2. 'Praxis'-action that was informed by knowledge and linked to values. Knowledge was not for the sake of knowledge only but was primarily to be used as a tool to empower people to impact their world. For example,

in the Jacobin discussion group in Lexington, Kentucky, rich discussions occurred when young white intellectuals were joined by activists from the community and they shared knowledge derived from their own experience. This resulted from both groups learning. One of the most dynamic sessions was when we discussed gentrification;

3. Building hope for the oppressed. As consciousness is increased, society can be transformed. The knowledge we seek we seek because we want to change the world. Knowledge can be empowering. Knowledge provides an explanation of why human beings are in the situations they are in;

4. The importance of linking education with the real world experiences of the students. This means that real world political campaigns and struggles should inform discussions addressing questions such as what was learned, what worked, and what didn't work? In which ways can these experiences be compared and contrasted with other struggles elsewhere and from the past? And,

5. Trying to highlight and minimize the differences between teachers and learners. Each participant in any study group brings to the group a lifetime of experience. Economic survival, political activism, and organizational commitments, all framed by various educational backgrounds, ensure the richness of discussion and debate.

Such practice aids in what has been described as "organic intellectual" development. Gramsci describes organic intellectuals as a designation whose function in society is to organize, administer, direct, educate or in other ways lead people. Both Gramsci and Friere are describing a method to use when organizing a social group to oppose the dominant group in a society. Both authors rely heavily on dialectics as the organizing structure for the arguments they make to describe both the theory and the practice.

(See Heather Clayton, "From the Ideological to the Concrete: Ideas from Paulo Friere, Understanding by Design and the Ontario Curriculum and Their Implications to Layered Curriculum," http://www.help4teachers. com/heatherpaper.htm).

Goals and Next Steps for SEP

Recommendation 1.

We need to keep what does work. We suggest that the SEP continue its 4th Monday topical discussions. We need to explore the reasons for the limited participation, perhaps surveying the membership for ideas about how to improve the readings and discussions to address specific needs.

To make a greater impact we need to

- Involve more people in our discussions.

- Find out why more people do not participle. (Other national discussions draw 50 to hundreds of people).

- Make an effort to broaden the ranks of those who attend, participate, and listen. Design the 4th Monday sessions to assist people who set up local study groups.

- Use the Online University of the Left, thereby, training others to do the same, as a source of materials for the local study groups.

Recommendation 2.

Every area should organize a reading group that has discussions based upon articles from, for example, the Jacobin (https://www.jacobinmag. com/reading-groups/), Monthly Review, In These Times, and other socialist or progressive publications, such as CCDS Links, which is available electronically. For example, Jacobin reading groups have already been created in various locations. The Socialist Education Project could assist in connecting activists with the appropriate literature and possible participants in various areas.

Recommendation 3.

We need to do more and deeper theoretical work. We propose development of an on-line study group or groups that are more in depth and theoretical. (While the theoretical and deep discussions are important most people will not be able to use them until we provide metaphors through storytelling (personal experiences) that illustrate the theory. Many educators understand that experiences are metaphors and thus enrich discussions.

For example, Gramsci notes that, "The apparatus of state coercive power which 'legally' enforces discipline on those groups who do not 'consent' either actively or passively. This apparatus is, however, constituted for the whole society in anticipation of moments of crisis of command and direction when spontaneous consent has failed" (A Gramsci Reader, p.

307). A recent example is police killings of people (predominantly Black men). In this case, the 'apparatus' (policing practices) is breaking down because of technology that allows the most affected groups to have their experiences expressed. The experiences describe the crisis. The crisis is informing the public, which is now demanding new ideas of policing as the current model has spontaneously failed. Such an understanding of pedagogy informs the organic intellectual because the in-depth and theoretical discussions can assist in groups of people who together form a cause to help end or reduce oppression(s).

We need to explore dialectical teaching methods both theoretically derived from the Marxist heritage and contemporary educator/activists. Dialectical pedagogy started with Hegel and the material.

There have been several areas suggested to do this deeper theoretical study.

1. Use 'The Struggle for a Substantive Democracy' for groups to begin their discussions, so that analysis and thinking, using dialectics, informs future discussions.

2. Twenty-First Century Socialism. What is it or how do we build it? What do we mean by socialism? How is it created? Dialectics (Marx or Hegel/Marx) must be a central part of this work as the starting point for pedagogy for use in the study group. For example, topics need to include: the spiral of learning, contradictions, unity of opposites, etc.

3. A study of African American history in the US. We will soon have published the Democracy Charter Study Guide and this can be utilized to facilitate this efforts. Also, there are some excellent books to read, The Half That Has Never Been Told, and Slavery by Another Name.

4. Views and positions from participants in the Black Lives Matter movement.

5. A study of the relationship between European and Indigenous cultures. For example, the relationship between the former Soviet government, the CPUSSR and the Native peoples of northern Russia should be explored

Recommendation 4.

Types of study groups could include a number of scenarios where studies take place on different levels. One set of classes can be conceived of for a broader progressive community, another specifically for people who come from the Left and who may be interested in joining CCDS or finally, a group for theoretical studies.

Recommendation 5:

SEP study groups, committees and chapters of CCDS should play a larger role in summing up work in their areas so as to provide leadership to the organization as well as the mass movement. For example, the Days of Grace Movement, that began in Charleston, SC after a blatantly racist killing of nine beautiful people. The demand for a reduction in gun violence was a direct spinoff of this movement and the movement is beginning to incorporate a public health perspective to help people understand ways to reduce gun violence in a society where guns are very readily available.

Recommendation 6:

Make better use of the Online University of the Left in all of its work.

1. Do education among our membership on how to use this.

2. Use the information in all of the above.

3. Work with NCC members and chapter members on how to use this effectively.

4. Hold an online discussion on how to use this good resource.

5. Utilize materials for discussion at local book stores.

6. And, encourage teachers to use these resources as appropriate.

These are six recommendations we can take to expand and deepen our revolutionary education work in CCDS. We have many fine activists in our organization. We should strive to change some of those activists into organizers and those organizers into organic intellectuals. We should do this in the spirit of left unity. We call on members to join us on the SEP to help us accomplish these tasks.

Planning a 21st Century 'New World Order:' More Violence, Environmental Destruction, and Human Suffering

By Harry Targ

From a Washington Post editorial, May 21, 2016:

HARDLY A day goes by without evidence that the liberal international order of the past seven decades is being eroded. China and Russia are attempting to fashion a world in their own illiberal image...This poses an enormous trial for the next U.S. president. We say trial because no matter who takes the Oval Office, it will demand courage and difficult decisions to save the liberal international order. As a new report from the Center for a New American Security points out, this order is worth saving, and it is worth reminding ourselves why: It generated unprecedented global prosperity, lifting billions of people out of poverty; democratic government, once rare, spread to more than 100 nations; and for seven decades there has been no cataclysmic war among the great powers. No wonder U.S. engagement with the world enjoyed a bipartisan consensus.

The Washington Post editorial quoted above clearly articulates the dominant view envisioned by US foreign policy elites for the years ahead. It in effect constitutes a synthesis of the "neocon" and the "liberal interventionist" wings of the ruling class. In my judgment, with all our attention on primaries, who goes to which bathrooms, and other mystifications, a New Cold War is being planned. Only this time it will have even greater consequences for global violence and devastation of the environment than the first one.

The Post's vision of a New World Order built upon a reconstituted United States military and economic hegemony has been a central feature of policymaking at least since the end of World War II even though time after time it has suffered setbacks: from defeat in Vietnam, to radical decolonization across the Global South, and to the rise of competing poles of power in Asia, the Middle East, Latin America, and even Europe. And despite recent setbacks, grassroots mass mobilizations against neoliberal globalization and austerity policies have risen everywhere, even in the United States. The Washington Post speaks to efforts to reassemble the same constellation of political forces, military resources, and concentrated wealth, that, if anything, is greater than at any time since the establishment of the US "permanent war economy" after the last World War.

Recent US diplomacy illustrates the application of the vision. President Obama remains committed to trade agreements that will open the doors in every country to penetration by the 200 corporations and banks that dominate the global economy. He continues to expand military expenditures and to authorize the development of new generations of nuclear weapons (at the same time as he visits the site of the dropping of the first atomic bomb at Hiroshima). He engages aggressively in words, deeds, and provocative military moves against Russia and China.

Also, he recently visited Cuba, proclaiming the willingness of the United States to help that country shift its economic model to "free market" capitalism and "democracy." He then traveled to Argentina to give legitimacy to President Macri, recently elected advocate of that country's return to the neoliberal agenda. Meanwhile the United States encourages those who promote instability in Brazil, Venezuela, Bolivia, and Honduras and offers continuing support to the long-term violent politics of Colombia.

During the President's visit to Vietnam, he declared an end to the long-standing US arms embargo against that country and warmly supports that country's incorporation into the Trans Pacific Partnership. He hopes to construct a military coalition against China, even while criticizing Vietnam's record on human rights. After Vietnam Obama is scheduled to travel to Hiroshima at a time when new militarist currents have become more popular in Japan and while US troops continue to engage in violent behavior against citizens of Okinawa, where the US has a military base. In addition, US naval vessels patrol the South China Sea.

These trips have been paralleled by the President's historic trip to the Persian Gulf earlier this year, shoring up the ties with Saudi Arabia which have been a centerpiece of Middle East/Persian Gulf policy since President Roosevelt negotiated a permanent partnership with that country in the spring of 1945. President Obama has resumed a slow but steady escalation of "boots on the ground" in Iraq, continued support for rebels fighting ISIS and at the same time the government of Syria. And to carry out the mission of reconstituting US hegemony drone strikes and bombing missions target enemies in multiple countries in the Middle East and North Africa.

The increasing contradictions of finance and industrial capital grow on a worldwide basis and masses of people in many countries are standing up against the imposition of austerity policies. Also it is becoming clearer to all classes that the natural environment is in peril. But the Washington Post calls for a return to the US global policy that emerged after World War II and which benefited banks, multinational corporations, and the military-industrial complex as millions of people died in war. Only this time, the US imperial model is less likely to succeed, irrespective of the results of the November, 2016 election.

Harry Targ is a professor at Purdue University and a member of the National Executive Committee of CCDS.

Conference of the Parties 21: What was achieved, what are the challenges to the Climate Justice movement?

By David Schwartzman

Introduction

How much the global climate will warm by 2100 is critical to whether catastrophic climate change (C3) will become a reality in the lifetimes of our children and grandchildren or not. Now many climate scientists are arguing that anything more than 1.5 deg C above the pre-industrial level will be too much to prevent C3. We have only about 0.5 deg C left to keep below this limit.

Conference of the Parties 21 (COP21) for the first time recognized the 1.5 deg C limit as a goal, but the Paris agreement falls far short of achieving this limit in projected commitments from the world's biggest polluters.

Nevertheless, we still have a small window of opportunity to keep warming below 1.5 deg C, but only if carbon emissions are curbed sooner and more radically. This article outlines the challenges ahead for the climate and energy justice movement.

COP 21 just concluded its meeting on December 12 in Paris. COP 21 was the 21st meeting of the Conference of the Parties to the United Nations Framework on Climate Change, a process started in 1992 at the Rio Earth Summit. Climate justice activists generally had very sober expectations of its outcome, although this COP meeting was the first at which virtually all countries will at least submit their national plans with regard to climate change, subject to periodic review.

What did the COP 21 process achieve? Significance of the 1.5 degree C target

To summarize:

1) Agreed to goal of keeping global temperature increase "well below" 2 deg C and to pursue efforts to limit it to 1.5 deg C warming above pre-industrial by 2100. (Goal but no penalties for failing to achieve INDCs, the Intended National Determined Contributions to curb carbon emissions over a projected time period).

For more information on the results of COP21 go to: http://newsroom. unfccc.int/unfccc-newsroom/finale-cop21/

"The fact that the accord prominently mentions the 1.5 °C target is a huge victory for vulnerable countries, says Saleemul Huq, director of the International Centre for Climate Change and Development in Dhaka, Bangladesh. "Coming into Paris, we had all of the rich countries and all of the big developing countries not on our side," says Huq, an adviser to a coalition of least-developed nations. "In the 14 days that we were here, we managed to get all of them on our side." (Nature Dec. 17, 2015).

2) 176 nations including the biggest greenhouse gas polluters, China, U.S. and EU, made specific commitments (INDCs) to eventually curb their greenhouse gas emissions, as well as to peak them as soon as possible.

(Note: Roughly 60 percent of greenhouse gas emissions come from fossil-fuel use, with coal, natural gas (due to methane leakage into the atmosphere), and tar sands oil having the highest carbon footprint. Conventional liquid oil has the lowest carbon footprint, about three-fourths that of coal. (The other greenhouse gases derived from human activity include nitrous oxide, the breakdown product of nitrate fertilizer, with carbon dioxide and methane also coming from agriculture.)

3) This agreement requires a review of progress towards increasing their INDCs every five years, in a transparent process.

("Each Party shall communicate a nationally determined contribution every five years ...and any relevant decisions of the Conference of the Parties serving as the meeting of the Parties to the Paris Agreement..", p. 22, ADOPTION OF THE PARIS AGREEMENT, December 12, 2015; You can download a pdf of this treaty at: http://unfccc.int/essential_background/ library/items/3599.php?such=j&symbol=FCCC/CP/2015/L.9#beg)

4) Agreement included a commitment to $100 billion a year in climate finance for developing countries by 2020, and to further finance in the future.

5) The Paris Agreement is nearly universal, and as such is a symbolic step towards global cooperation and a more peaceful world.

How far is the Paris Agreement from an effective prevention program to avoid Catastrophic Climate Change?

Based on sum of INDC commitments: 2.7 to 3.5 deg C warming above pre-industrial by 2100 instead of agreed goal of keeping global temperature increase "well below" 2 deg C and to pursue efforts to limit it to 1.5 deg C.

In the Introduction to the treaty itself we find: "much greater emissions reduction efforts will be required" to meet even the 2-degree target.

According to the IPCC holding warming to 2 °C will probably require emissions to be cut by 40–70% by 2050 compared with 2010 levels, Achieving the 1.5 °C target would require substantially larger emissions cuts — of the order of 70–95% by 2050.

Since the Paris Agreement doesn't fully take effect until 2020 the chance to achieve the 1.5-degree goal will have already gone, unless all of the world's largest economies dramatically change course.

Some climate scientists/activists assessments:

Jim Hansen, retired NASA climate scientist: "It's a fraud really, a fake," .. "It's just bullshit for them to say: 'We'll have a 2C warming target and then try to do a little better every five years.' It's just worthless words. There is no action, just promises. As long as fossil fuels appear to be the cheapest fuels out there, they will be continued to be burned."

Patrick Bond, climate justice leader from South Africa: "Since 2009, US State Department chief negotiator Todd Stern successfully drove the negotiations away from four essential principles: ensuring emissions-cut commitments would be sufficient to halt runaway climate change; making the cuts legally binding with accountability mechanisms; distributing the burden of cuts fairly based on responsibility for causing the crisis; and making financial transfers to repair weather-related loss and damage following directly from that historic liability.

Washington elites always prefer 'market mechanisms' like carbon trading instead of paying their climate debt even though the US national carbon market fatally crashed in 2010."

What is the way forward for Climate Justice?

Rather than immobilizing the climate justice movement from the recognition of the huge challenges unaddressed in the COP21 agreement, indications so far point to a reenergizing process as a result, building on its recent victories such as the rejection of the X-L Keystone pipeline by President Obama and the actions of cities around the world to take more aggressive steps to curb their greenhouse gas emissions and transition to renewable energy supplies.

I suggest the following issues be put front and center:

1) The huge subsidies going to fossil fuels (IMF study: $5 trillion/year), with indirect costs including health impacts from air pollution (3-7 million die every year), with a goal to nationalize and decentralize with community management and ownership clean energy supplies in a full transition to wind/solar power.

2) The Military Industrial (Fossil Fuel Nuclear State Terror and Surveillance) Complex as block to achieving global cooperation for rapid curb on greenhouse gas emissions and a full global transition to wind/solar power. The Pentagon/Nato is the instrumental arm of Imperial foreign policy of the MIC, so while the Pentagon is going "green" with respect to energy conservation and use of renewables it is simply "greenwashing its Imperial role. The Pentagon's recognition of the growing security threat from climate change reinforces the Imperial Agenda and military spending.

For the Green New Deal

Yes, of course there are critical contradictions within capital regarding energy policy, and the Green New Deal strategy must capture the "solar" faction of capital into a multi-class alliance to force demilitarization and termination of the perpetual war dynamic to have any hope of implementing a C3 prevention in time. Does any socialist believe that this prevention program can be realized as long as the State Terror apparatus is locked in the vicious cycle of violence with its useful enemy, its terrorist antagonist?

As I concluded my Jacobin interview, the "vision of a knowledge-based, democratic, and socialist transition is building in passion and intensity, but it must confront its blind spots and weaknesses. In particular it must focus on forcing the dissolution of the military-industrial complex — a goal which is simultaneously a requirement for preventing catastrophic climate change and removing a major barrier to an ecosocialist path and the end of capitalism on our planet."

To sum up, CCDS's strategy remains very relevant: Build movement for a Global Green New Deal

I recommend an excellent resource: Trade Unions for Energy Democracy:

http://unionsforenergydemocracy.org/

Also see my website with Peter Schwartzman, my older son:
http://www.solarutopia.org

For more from my perspective check out this Jacobin interview, December 1, 2015:

https://www.jacobinmag.com/2015/12/cop-21-paris-climate-change-global-warming-fossil-fuels/)

For a more general documented version see: http://www.cnsjournal.org/cop21-achievements-and-challenges-to-the-climate-justice-movement/

David Schwartzman, dschwartzman@gmail.com, is a biochemist, professor, and a leader in the climate justice movement.

Spirituality in Left Education: A Discussion Document

By Tony Kaliss

Introduction

The purpose of this paper is to suggest that spirituality is the critical factor in determining how humans will act in the real world and, therefore, spirituality must be a critical factor in a socialist education. However, the Left, especially the Marxist Left, has had an especially difficult time dealing with the nature of spirituality. I suggest not understanding spirituality has much to do with the systemic failure of the European Left to establish a working socialist system and the Left's fragmentation and marginalization. In focusing on spirituality, I'm in no way downplaying other essential topics of a socialist education. But, as a critically important factor in human behavior it has been overlooked and needs recognition of its role in regard to all the topics.

Participation in the Socialist Education Project of the CCDS encouraged me to get my thinking down as follows. Also, a while back I did prepare a paper exploring the relationship of the Left and spirituality generally (see below for a link).

Nature and function of Spirituality

Socialism and Communism—one meaning of "-ism" at the end of an English word means a belief in what precedes the "-ism". An "-ist" is an individual who shares a particular "-ism". What humans believe at a given time is fundamental to what they will actually do. The belief in the "social" and the "communal" has been the fundamental motivator in my life's activity for over 55 years. Facts, real or imagined, may be used to support a belief, but my basic point is that belief, not the facts, is the actual motivator. Belief, however, is only one expression of something fundamental to human behavior namely Spirituality. Spirituality is the filter through which all that exists, outside us, reaches the inside. Certainly there is an "objective" reality, a material base, outside us but, that reality reaches us humans only through the filter of our spirituality. Therefore, for humans, spirituality is every bit as important as the material base for understanding what motivates and changes people's real actual behavior.

Spirituality includes a complex of emotions, feelings and intuitive reactions that are experienced as a combination of mental and physical interactions. The overall spiritual orientation or reaction may be influenced by observations about events, observations that may be factually right or wrong. But, spirituality itself does factually exist and is fundamental to human motivation. In other words, what a person believes to exist in their imagination may not exist in fact but because that spiritual belief becomes the basis for behavior in the real world, spirituality becomes a very real factor in that real world.

For example, what counts is not the factual possibility of obtaining an aerial view of Santa Claus's workshop at the North Pole, but how the story of Santa Claus influences the spiritual reaction about gift giving which can and does affect the facts of human behavior. The spiritual is very practical. Not only is it fundamental to human motivations, it is the factor that unites mind and body. Feelings of connection or disconnection have profound influences on the very chemistry of the brain and body. It has been shown, for example, how feelings of stress affect us down to the cellular level. Overthrow capitalism for the sake of your cellular health.

Therefore, a socialist education must include the study and understanding of the role of the spirituality that is at the core of a belief in Socialism and Commun(e)-ism. By the same reasoning it is equally important to understand the nature of spiritual beliefs opposing socialism and communism. A socialist education process that recognizes the reality of spirituality and the very real practical effects of spirituality is an education that provides a basis for a much deeper, broader, more flexible understanding of today's complex globalized world. Indeed, in today's world a broader approach is needed than the usual focus on the facts of why capitalism needs to be replaced by socialism.

Focusing on the role of spirituality is in no way meant to ignore or downplay the role of the facts about socialism, capitalism or any other social (or natural) phenomena. Indeed, as noted, spirituality has a factual existence of its own. However, the Left generally and the Marxist left in particular, has a special problem in regard to spirituality because the Left's assumption that the material base is fundamental to human motivation has been interpreted to deemphasize the role of spirituality. Additionally, there is a strongly held chain of beliefs that equates spirituality with religion which, in turn, is seen as a belief in a God or spirits which don't exist, and, even worse, religion is often used as a tool of oppression. This logic can lead to a very negative view of spirituality and certainly to an inadequate understanding of its nature and function. My point is that religion is one of the possible expressions of spirituality not the other way round.

The Left's difficulty in dealing with the subject of spirituality is confounded by the fact that part of the Left's positions concerning it are themselves beliefs that operate at the spiritual level. Beliefs, as an expression of the spiritual, are very strongly held and can operate at both the conscious and unconscious levels. So, a strongly held belief that spirituality is about something that doesn't exist or is something apart from the material base is a belief that can make it difficult to see that the issue even exists or that it is an issue that needs to be considered.

I suggest that the difficulty in dealing with spirituality is a direct result of the historical context the European Left developed in. I suggest this is at the core of the failure of European-based Left theories and practice in the socialist countries and the divisions and marginalization of the Left in the present day. Moreover, the difficulty that the Left has in dealing with the spiritual factor, is at the core of why the Left's explanations of what happened to the European left remain very incomplete and shallow.

A Socialist education framework generally.

Humans are all about relationships. The most fundamental relationships are those between the human mind and body, between humans, and between humans and the environment around them. An effective socialist education framework needs to focus on those relationships and must include the spiritual dynamic by which humans come to see and understand those relationships. In other words, there is both the practical objective reality of those relationships and the spiritual processes by which humans come to understand and, most importantly, act in regard to those relationships. The essential question for humans is what kind of life do you want to live? This raises the related questions of what kind of life are you living now and how do you continue or achieve the kind of life you would like to live? These are at the same time both spiritual and practical questions. They are the basis of moral practices for the better or the worse.

Fifty years of work on issues between Native peoples and non-Natives, most especially of European origin, led to the following model of their interaction, which I believe has wider application as a model of two fundamentally opposed spiritual/practical ways of life.

I wanted a model that was concise but from which complexity can be spun out and I wanted the terms of that model to combine the practical and the spiritual in the sense that the terms could be factually examined but at the same time represent a spiritual approach to those facts. The model is as follows:

Native European

Sharing vs.Taking Without Giving (TWG)

Connection vs.Disconnection

Harmony vs.Disharmony

I believe that one of the greatest strengths of this model is that it allows an approach to all aspects of the complexity of today's globalized world. I mean this in two regards. One, this model can be applied to all aspects of human relationships, individual, social, political, religious, economic, environmental and so on. And second, in as much as we live in a globalized world we cannot avoid dealing with complex social-economic relationships that take forms that go beyond the borders of one country and beyond the dichotomy, as important as it is, between capitalism and socialism. Because the model applies to all aspects of human relationships it can also show how those relationships are themselves interrelated.

The individual is indeed political and vice versa. Relationships among humans cannot be separated from human relationships with the environment. One of the major failures in the socialist countries has been the failure to recognize and understand that all these relationships are interrelated. The successful construction of a socialist economy, for example, cannot be separate from the nature of the relationships between male and female, from the relationship of humans with the environment, or the relationship of the ruling Party to the people regarding human and democratic rights.

In today's world a focus on just socialism versus capitalism is much too narrow. It provides no way to understand what is happening in China or India or the corruption that is the basis of social-economic situations in a number of countries. Even in the countries that are distinctly capitalist we need the flexibility to present the situation as it actually looks and feels to people in each specific country and situation.
Some comments on the model above.

I described this model in some detail as applied to the Native-European interaction in a conference presentation a couple of years ago and then made use of it in the paper on the Left and spirituality mentioned above. Both are available from the links below. But, a few explanatory comments should be made here. First, by European, I refer to Europeans and their descendants—Russian, English, Spanish, Euro-American, Euro-Australian, etc.

Second, the arrows are meant to indicate the dynamic interaction vertically and horizontally of the components of the model. Horizontally, the two sides represent fundamentally opposite ways of relating, factually and spiritually, whether it be of individuals or social systems, political parties or religions, or Natives and Europeans. Vertically, each side is an interrelation of three factors. Sharing is based on a recognition of Connection and both practiced together lead to Harmony.

Lastly, concerning Natives and Europeans, I am in no way suggesting that on one side we have noble Natives who share everything, and, on the other, savage Europeans who take everything. On both sides there are those who do not share the overall ethic.

Five specific education topics.

The role of spirituality needs to be a major component of all our presentations in the sense that the subject matter, in one way or another, is involved with the relationships between the human mind and body, between humans, and/or between humans and the environment. An excellent example is the subject matter of racism and sexism, which cannot be separate from how these issues are experienced at a spiritual level. Another is that climate change is really about human change in regard to the three relationships. The five specific topics below can be addressed in a variety of formats-courses, workshops, readings, internet discussions, etc.

Topic 1. The nature of spirituality.

The main purpose is to show how human spirituality functions as the medium though which humans come to be aware of, to understand, and, most importantly, to act in regard to the three fundamental interactions humans deal with as noted above. Of course, all three of these interactions are interrelated and influence each other. There are a multitude of real life interesting and important examples that can explored. An example is how taking without giving (TWG) versus sharing have very different spiritual effects that affect the physical body down to the cellular level which, in turn, influences the spiritual state of mind. Based on this understanding, we can explore some of the ways that humans have made use, deliberately and consciously or not, of specific actions and/or arguments aimed at influencing the spiritual state of mind in order to get individuals or groups of people to act in certain ways. For most Native peoples, the use of ceremonies, stories, vision quests, dance and song all have the very deliberate purpose of influencing people at the spiritual level to act in desired ways.

Learning how to use the framework of spirituality in general, and my model in particular, to gain a greater awareness of what is happening in a globalized world and how it relates to particular local concerns is the objective. It is impossible for one person or one movement to address all the issues and it is true that real change must begin in one's own backyard. But, it is essential while working on the local to understand how this affects and is affected by what is happening globally. Explore how and why the Left has had such difficulty in dealing with spirituality. There are two reasons for this difficulty, which would need to be explored in some detail. This is a subject that also must be addressed in topics 3 and 4 below.

One, the Left has confused spirituality with religion and since organized religion has often been used to support the TWG of the ruling class spirituality got tossed out, downplayed, or just plain got a bad rap as being part of something that was being used to confuse ordinary people and to blind them to the facts of an oppressive system. The second reason flows from the Left's, and especially the "scientifically" based Left, acceptance of a fundamental assumption of the European knowledge system known as Science that it can deal objectively with the facts of reality and that this ability allows it to know the truth, which makes it the most advanced and, therefore, most superior to all human knowledge systems. That fundamental assumption, and the notion of superiority that goes with it, have far more to do with the goals of the upcoming Capitalist system, which wanted great quantities of facts about the real world to better practice TWG apart from any concerns with ethical or spiritual ramifications of what they were doing with those facts and which necessarily saw itself and its viewpoints as superior in every way as justification for TWG.

Topic 2 Racism, sexism, ethnicity and belief systems.

In today's world these topics are of great importance in how humans relate to each other personally and politically. Spirituality plays a vital and critical role in regard to these topics. There is a wealth of examples to draw from worldwide. The stress here is not so much on the details of how issues of racism, sexism and/or ethnicity and beliefs show themselves. Rather it is on how people, individually or in groups, react to and understand these issues. In the U.S. the right wing has been much more aware than the Left of the importance of spirituality in influencing people's views on these issues. On the other hand, spirituality was and remains a fundamental motivating force in the Civil Rights movement.

Topic 3. The failure of the European-left to build lasting mass movements in general and the critical failure in the building of a socialist alternative in specific countries.

This is an absolutely fundamental and critical issue that has been avoided, shallowly understood and not deeply investigated. Yet it is critical for the future of the Left. To put it plainly–if you're so smart why ain't you rich? Why should people now believe the Left or its analyses considering these failures? I suggest these failures are directly related to the failure to understand the nature and role of spirituality because the failures have their roots at the spiritual level. In other words, if the role of spirituality is not understood then the centrality of its role in the failures cannot be understood. This discussion includes not only what happened in the former European socialist countries, but also what is happening in those that still claim to be socialist. The flip side of this topic is how, after understanding the failures, does the Left build lasting, broad and influential movements that do recognize the role of spirituality. This overlaps with Topics 1 and 4.

Topic 4. Marxist philosophy generally and its application to the understanding of the evolution of human history.

A focus here is on how Marxist philosophy has up to now and should in the future deal with the nature and role of human spirituality. Fifty-five years of political activity still leave me feeling that the fundamentals of Marxist philosophy remain the most valid and useful approach to understanding the processes of the universe both human and otherwise. That includes the nature and role of spirituality. However, a valid approach does not mean every application of Marxist dialectics to specific processes is correct. There's the broad but true generality that the universe is infinite and human knowledge is always finite, which means our understanding of specific processes are always subject to correction. In particular, there are several areas of critical importance where Marxist analysis has been incomplete or in error. One serious lack of understanding concerns how the notion of the material base, as the determining factor in human behavior, was applied in a way that is fundamentally flawed regarding the role of spirituality. Another is the assumption of European superiority that has accompanied the notion of progressive stages of history. The third is the idea that the European belief system known as Science is the most superior viewpoint for knowing the world based on the idea that it is possible for humans to deal objectively with the facts of the real world and in so doing it becomes the one worldview that can really know truth.

Spirituality. One sign of the Left's difficulty with spirituality is that it is hard to pin down precisely how it is understood. But it is clear that the Left has tended to see spirituality as something distinct from the material base and, in a sense, opposed to it in that spirituality is seen as preventing people from seeing the real facts of the material base. As I suggest above, we need to show how spirituality is not only part of the material base but that it is an essential part in that it concerns how humans do understand the facts.

European superiority. This must include challenging and changing the notion that Europeans are the most advanced people when it comes to progress towards a human society based on sharing, connection and harmony. There is significant and interesting debate on how (or if) Marx and Engels changed over time on this issue. But, there is no question that subsequent Marxist movements have held a stages of history model in which Europe ends up as the most advanced stage of history, the European working class as the most advanced social force in that stage, and the Communist party as the most advanced representative of the most advanced social class. This assumption of European superiority is actually a spiritually based belief that the Left inherited from European history. It has led to deadly contradictions and enormous harm. It is seen in everything from how the ruling Parties treated critics, to the treatment of the environment, and, as I have seen from many years of work with Native peoples, to an attitude of superiority from the Left that has been very harmful to Native peoples.

Science, objectivity and superiority. I commented on this above, but it should also be noted that the idea that it was possible for humans to know the world objectively led to the belief that European Science was the most superior worldview for knowing the world, which logically led to the conclusion that European Science had the truth and, finally, to extremely destructive arguments that the Left has the true scientific analysis and therefore knows the real truth. Interestingly, these quarrels have all the flavor of holders of strongly held spiritual beliefs who feel their beliefs as being challenged. This remains an ongoing problem in bringing about a working Left unity. A problem, I suggest, who's dynamic can only be understood by understanding the operation of spirituality.

Topic 5. The nature and operation of the capitalist, socialist and communist social-economic systems.

It is essential that this include, as a major component, how working people (and also the ruling class) have reacted spiritually to the facts of these systems. It needs to deal with the diverse ways in which TWG actually works in the wide variety of situations worldwide, and the equally diverse ways that the affected people (and the environment) react to oppose the TWG. The actual workings of the various social-economic processes in today's globalized and inter-active world vary greatly. The basics of the capitalist versus socialist social economic systems as they are usually presented while true often do not take into account the very different and complex ways that processes of sharing versus TWG are actually taking place in countries as varied as the United States or China. The spiritual factor concerns the ways in which these varied processes are perceived, felt and understood by the different social-economic groupings. Again, there's a world's worth of interesting and important examples of these processes.

The social-economic systems of the world's Indigenous peoples must be included. Marxist analysis has tended to ignore them due to viewing them as "primitive" communists or just plain backward unscientific peoples who needed the guidance of advanced European Communists (as I saw for myself in the former USSR). In fact, the worldwide experience over centuries of time that Native peoples have had in making use of spirituality as a factor in maintaining a viable working model of a sharing society is of vital importance to the discussion of building such a society in today's world on both practical and spiritual levels.

Follow-up. I consider the above as a work in progress and so I welcome comments, suggestions, corrections, etc. I can be reached at tkaliss@ gmail.com.

Download links for papers

The Left and Spirituality—A Practical Question, https://www.dropbox.com/s/to3q0htqmqldnnz/Kaliss-Left%26Spirituality%2012-18-2014.pdf?dl=0

From the Practical to the Spiritual and Back: A Model for the Interaction of European and Native Societies, https://www.dropbox.com/s/m99p-myt7zpu2hq2/Kaliss-ANS1-Paper-Final.pdf?dl=

Tony Kaliss has worked with and studied Native people's for 50 years.

Comments on Pre-convention Documents

Yuseff Lomas

CCDS California Prison Chapter member

I think we need to be more visible in the communities we are trying to affect, particularly the working-class and low income communities. They need to know that we exist and that we offer an alternative to the current societal structure. I believe that can be achieved by engaging in activities and campaigns that highlight our socialist values and show people who we are and what we are about. If we get out there in the trenches and show them what socialism looks like, our message will have a bigger impact. I think movements like Occupy Wall Street and Black Lives Matter are good places to seek out new members. They are high profile and offer maximum exposure of their ideas to the public. They also have a lot of young people with fresh ideas. There is a big movement in San Francisco now that is protesting several police shootings. They're trying to get the police chief fired. These are the kinds of movements we should be involved in, if we aren't already.

I got the book you sent, "The New Jim Crow." It's riveting. It never occurred to me that racism was simply a tool that capitalist society uses to manipulate its inhabitants. I have a couple of proposals for CCDS to explore, if that's possible. One is setting up community gardens in urban, low income communities. It would give people a chance to see what socialism looks like. People working together for the benefit of the people. That will help show a lot of people that there is an alternative to the current system under which we live. I would also like to discuss voter registration drives in urban and rural areas. A lot of people are unaware of the impact that they can make locally and nationally if enough people vote.

Editor's response: Thank you Yuseff for those good suggestions. CCDS members were involved in the Occupy Wall Street movement and the Black Lives Matter movement (see the article by Frank Chapman and Aislinn Pulley in Chicago, for example). We could have done more (we need to grow), and especially improve our efforts to recruit people; it's an issue we are discussing now. Thank you for bringing up all your suggestions. It helps inform us of how important it is to be active in the community and in these grassroots movements.

Brandon Rivers

CCDS California Prison Chapter member

Thank you for the opportunity to share my thoughts with CCDS. I know the upcoming CCDS convention is very serious since our goal is complete solidarity with the masses of people. Many people find it difficult to understand what we are saying and teaching, even though they are searching for the same goals as the CCDS. They don't possess the vocabulary to articulate that truth. Hence, they turn to alternative forms of rebellion, no matter how erroneous they may be.

Too many people what we speak and teach is "jargon." It is akin to the scientist attempting to teach elementary school children scientific principles using the same terminology employed in the laboratory. Meanwhile, the elitists who fund and control the media and mainstream educational curriculum intentionally teach the people blatant lies but they do it in a simple language that is easily understood by everyone.

What we say is honest and true. But I feel as though the complexity and richness of our message cannot be fully digested by those who need it the most when we speak in a manner that the listener cannot understand. We must speak to them in a way that they will comprehend. I would like to suggest that CCDS consider setting up classes were members can learn how to explain our ideas in a way that is directed to the masses of people, at the level that they are on, such as the average worker or unemployed young person. I hope this suggestion isn't taken lightly as I speak from the experience of being one of those people, even though I did good in school. I never had anyone to simplify these concepts to me until I gained a" higher education" in prison. We need elementary school age children and their parents on board just as much as we need aware adult workers and college students. Thank you, and peace.

Melvin Jones

CCDS California Prison Chapter member

I've been reading "The New Jim Crow" book that you sent me. To learn about the racial caste system in our country was a real eye opener. I don't think too many people understand how important the divisions are that are based on wealth and occupation. Those divisions are one of the most increasing forms of racism. Look at all the police brutality and gang violence. We have to deprogram how both sides think. My plan is to get out of this hell-hole so I can try to give back to my community. I have been campaigning for Bernie Sanders. My mom, grandma and lady friend promise to vote for Bernie Sanders on my account. I'm glad CCDS reached out to me. It has opened my eyes and changed my life.

Section 3: CCDS's Work and Working with Our Allies

Fighting Racism

Editor's Note:The following article is divided into two parts. In the first part each one of the authors, all inmates in California prisons, describe events in their lives that had a big impact on them, and how they searched for and found answers to the racism and other injustices they experienced and witnessed. Each person describes how his association with CCDS transformed his thinking and why he joined CCDS. The second part describes the process that unfolded that led to their joining. Lessons can be drawn from this piece regarding recruiting strategies.

Over 2.3 million people are behind bars in the US, the largest incarcerated population in the world. African American men comprise nearly 1 million of that number, more than the total number of prisoners in Argentina, Canada, England, Finland, Germany, India, Israel, Japan, and Lebanon combined.

African Americas (mostly men) comprise 35% of the US incarcerated population, yet comprise only 13% of the total population, revealing the racist nature of mass incarceration in the US. A Black male born in 1991 has a 29% chance of spending time in prison at some point in his life.

Since capitalism doesn't provide jobs or fair treatment for everyone, and especially not for African Americans, it has moved to criminalize them, lock them up, take them out of their communities, and deny them their humanity, future and vote.

The capitalist elite knows that the Black community is more critical of the abuses of capitalism and of political conservatives than any other sector of society, and is the most open to revolutionary change of any group.

California Prisoners form CCDS Chapter

Breaking from a Culture of Cruelty and Violence

By Alex Krehbiel

 My personal journey to join the Committees of Correspondence for Democracy and Socialism came about in a rather inauspicious way. As the son of two parents who are associated with CCDS, many might think my joining would be easy and natural. It wasn't.

Though I grew up in a home where the predatory nature of capitalism, racism, and capitalist society were explained, criticized and fought against, I was surrounded in the outside world by a vicious culture of individualism, selfishness, cruelty, and violence. While my parents were the exception, I none-the-less internalized the dominant divisive negative societal culture that predominated outside of my home as being the closest to social reality. I started from the standpoint that human nature was naturally selfish, so therefore we were all destined to rob, cheat and steal from one another. My parents tried hard to get me to see and live a different life, but I was too immersed in the culture of my peers on the street.

It wasn't until at the age of 27, during a second stint in prison, a maximum security prison, that my father -- who is on the National Coordinating Committee of CCDS, got through to me. He challenged my conception of human nature in a very forceful and emphatic way. He implored that I do some deep contemplative thinking about the kind of life I was leading, saying that if I continued I would end up spending my entire life in prison. He challenged me to think about the legacy I wanted to leave behind - a wasted life, or a constructive life. He challenged my thinking about human nature, debunking the negative stereotypes I held, and pointing to countless numbers of selfless warriors and political movements fighting for justice. He asked if I would look back on my life from my deathbed and feel content that I had led the best life possible, one that was in harmony with my fellow human beings.

That scared me. Here was the thought that there was another side of humanity that I could be a part of, and that I should think very hard and choose very wisely about which side would most likely fulfill my humanity. That was the first step toward a new life and new outlook, facilitated by a man, my Dad, who I loved and respected.

Both of my parents had been sending me books in prison about this new world, but now I began to read them more seriously. I read sociological, philosophical, and political texts in an insatiable manner. I read voluminous amounts of Marxist literature, theory and history. The discussions I have with both my parents are deep and meaningful. I started to understand that it is the social condition of men and women that determine their consciousness, while the ruling capitalist class works hard to make their ideas the ruling ideas. I realized that human beings are, foremost, social creatures who have the propensity for altruism and depravity, and it really matters what kind of socio-economic and objective social conditions and system predominates to determine which wins out. I realized that capitalist culture was the primary culprit in producing generation upon generation of self-destructive little capitalist caricatures (like gangsta's), as well as millions and millions of human beings the world over who were conditioned to seek their survival in an environment of class conflict and intense social pressure. I saw clearly that racism, oppression, and slavery were not inevitable manifestations germinating out of innate human proclivities. But that they were instead the inevitable manifestation of a specific mode of production, necessitated so that the exploitative and vicious system of capitalism, imperialism and colonialism could reproduce itself.

I saw that the other much more virtuous and fulfilling side of humanity was represented by Marx, Engels, Lenin, and so many others who were reaching for a better future: the rank-and-file workers, the community organizers in the inner cities, people of color oppressed by racism, the peasants in developing countries, and the exploited and have-nots everywhere. When they gain political consciousness, they become the protagonists in their own liberation, historically from slave revolts to the building of cooperative humane socialist societies. I also clearly saw that Marxist historical and dialectical materialism, when understood correctly, is not a dogma, but an open analytical approach to understanding our complex objective social, political and economic realities that allows us to effect real egalitarian revolutionary change in society.

I joined CCDS because it is an organization that is carrying the humanistic revolutionary banner for the creation of a new world -- a 21st century socialist world that will usher in universal human emancipation.

Marx said famously, philosophers have only interpreted the world, the point is to change it. I agree. I have had long talks with many of my fellow inmates. We began by holding study groups, and reading books by Marx, Lenin, and contemporary writers. I shared information about CCDS, including documents, reports, articles, and copies of the Mobilizer. A number have joined. Here are some of their stories, in their own words, and how we are building a CCDS chapter in the California prison system.

Capitalism Destroyed My Family

By Melvin Jones

Capitalism is founded on greed and personal gain. How can a democracy function under such an individually-based social structure? It cannot! Not productively and with longevity. That is why so many Americans are unhappy with the economy. That is why it's time for a social structural change.

Here is how the capitalist system destroyed my family. My mom was a single parent raising two children. She was able to get a job working in a factory in Los Angeles. The factory stored and shipped commodities. When she was employed there, she did fairly well financially. However, then she got laid off, and things started getting rough. We went from having, to have-nots. That can be tough on a child growing up. It's also tough on a single parent who doesn't have enough money to provide for her children. This hardship on my Mom, along with getting too little help from the government due to all the cutbacks in services, led her into depression.

She eventually descended into drug usage. To see my Mom fall from grace, hardened me as a kid. Now, with no supervision, I was out in the streets. At 11 years old, I was still clueless, and wanted to explore the world. Once I got exposed to gang-banging my life spiraled out of control.

The factory where my Mom had worked was shut down by the American owners so they could move their company overseas where they could get cheaper labor and make more money. I now understand that that is the nature of capitalism, to acquire more money without caring what happens to other people. That's how capitalism destroyed my life and my family. This should be alarming to everyone, and especially to my fellow Christians and people of other faiths. In the Bible, 1 Timothy 6:10 says: "for the love of money is a root of all kinds of evil..." So, capitalism should not be for a Christian.

When we were children in school we said the Pledge of Allegiance. It talked about how we were all united. They want us united in war, but when it comes to the government giving aid to the people, it all depends on what the return is. That's why capitalism needs to be abolished.

Here's an idea for CCDS members. You know how communities have neighborhood watch meetings? We should have socialism awareness meetings in our communities to learn how to protect ourselves and create a better life. In most urban communities, most Black folks don't think of politics until a presidential election. We tend to rally together only during tragedies. We need constant and consistent protection and rallies. That's why the Black Lives Matter movement is so important. It's raising people's consciousness. Police brutality, harassment, and unjustifiable arrests is what's been happening to African Americans since slavery.

How many people know about the Lease a Convict system, where they locked up Black folks for pretty much nothing so they could have bodies to work the chain gang. They would rent inmates to corporations. The inmates got nothing, and the government and corporations made money off the inmates' labor. That's called "modern day slavery."

That's why I joined CCDS because it is fighting to give the people the power to make choices in a real democracy. My goals are to learn more about socialism so I can enlighten my friends, family and community. We desperately need a change because capitalism is definitely not suitable, not now, not for the future, not ever!

Capitalism: Racism's First Born Son

By Joseph Williams

I want you to know that I am sending this letter with all of my love and the deepest respect for your movement as well as your cause. I truly think it's the most beautiful of things. I wish I was out to share in your passion and tenacity. My name is

Joseph Rheem Williams and I am a prisoner in California and will be until the mid-21st century.

I recently joined CCDS. My reason is CCDS's overall relation to the struggle of my people in this country. Socialism is the global answer to oppression. Since racism is capitalism's first born son, it was only natural for me to join ranks against a common enemy. Once you know better, it is your responsibility to do better. My way of living as well as my thought process was toxic. Not only to myself but also to society. When I became aware of this, I became open to new ideas and searched for answers. Answers for my pain. The pain of growing up a target of law enforcement. The pain of being in and out of Juvenile Hall for skipping school and other minor infractions. The pain of feeling like, regardless, my life just didn't matter.

What's crazy is that I no longer feel that pain. I lost in trial and was sentenced to twenty years in prison. I'm "okay." I've been incarcerated so frequently in my life that I understand it. But for my children, and my someday grandchildren, it's absolutely not okay! For them to be targeted or discriminated against or to think their lives mean nothing is not okay. That's another reason why I joined CCDS. For tomorrow's children.

I remember hearing one of the protesters say that the system is "broken." It's not broken. It's working better than ever. It was designed to keep us down. Until we get educated about the history of capitalism and arm ourselves with the weapons (knowledge) to overthrow it permanently we'll continue to be unjustly incarcerated, criminalized and murdered. It's capitalism pulling the strings of oppression. Black Lives really do Matter!

Unite the Exploited Many Against the Ruthless Few

By Brandon Rivers

Here's a shout out to all my fellow CCDS members. As we all share common goals and aspirations for our world and its future, we realize that only through unity can those goals be reached. A hand is comprised of four fingers and a thumb. When it is closed it forms a fist. In this state it can optimize its strength to its full potential, and act as one, unified and powerful.

The predatory, exploitative nature of capitalism tries to prevent this unity because it operates best for its masters by separating people by class, race, sex, status and state. The elite few who control and sustain capitalism have driven the entire world into an economic, social, environmental, and political crisis. By advocating "freedom and democracy" in words, their war-driven campaigns and slave-driving corporations exhibit their will to centralize the world's political and economic power into their own hands, just like the open dictators and tyrants they publicly rally against.

The elitism, racism, dictatorship and totalitarianism fostered by capitalism came before socialism. Socialism is a response to this exploitation and oppression. The problems faced by socialism and communism came from their enemies, the global capitalist nations under the IMF, for example. This does not change the solid ideological foundations of Marxism and socialism. Marxism and socialism are the only schools of thought that offer the masses an alternative understanding of reality, by helping us analyze and critique our current political and economic state of being. Our school curriculums, media, and the global market are all controlled by elite capitalists. Therefore, we have to study Marxism and socialism in order to understand our true reality. And we need the growth and consolidation of organizations like CCDS as our only way to realize our goal of a truly democratic and socialist country and world.

Anytime we must remind our government that "Black Lives Matter", and all lives for that matter, it is clear that we are under attack. The same elitist group that professes to ensure our well-being, is the same elitist group that is oppressing us: the capitalist class. That's why I and others have joined CCDS as a logical and necessary vehicle for the advancement of the exploited many against the ruthless few who use capital, propaganda, and violence to tyrannically rule us all.

Socialism Gives Power Back to the People

By Yuseff Lomas

For most of my life I've been content to sit around and complain about the plight of the young Black man in occupied America. Racism, police brutality, mass incarceration, economic inequality and subpar education are just some of the social injustices that the African American community deals with on a daily basis. With each passing day the situation grows more dire. Mass incarceration has decimated the number of Black males in society, and now police and others are killing Black men without fear of legal retribution. I could no longer just sit by idly while the conditions in society continue to erode.

That is what motivated me to join CCDS. I initially thought it would provide me with the tools I need to affect change in my community. But as I began to study and grow in my social consciousness I had a few very profound revelations. One was that Blacks don't have the market on oppression. All of the people who were not originally represented in the Declaration of Independence have been oppressed in some form or fashion. That includes women, Native Americans, Mexicans and poor people. I've come to understand that oppression doesn't stop at the borders of the US. It's a world-wide epidemic. In the words of Martin Luther King, an injustice anywhere is an injustice everywhere.

This brings me to another revelation. I was reading "Freedom is a Constant Struggle," by Angela Davis, where I was introduced to the philosophy of intersectionality. Before I was introduced to that concept I didn't like the idea of other groups tying their wagons to Black issues. I didn't understand the need for interconnections. But Angela Davis makes it clear that our shared experiences connect us in a number of different ways. These experiences make it easier to stand in solidarity with one another. The power is in the collective. As we continue to find those similarities that connect us we are able to advise one another when we see our peers facing a situation we have already gone through. Just as our brothers and sisters in occupied Palestine were able to advise the Black Lives Matter activists in Ferguson how to deal with the type of tear gas that they had previously used on Palestinian activists, we can use past experiences to teach one another.

By far, the most impactful revelation I had was the realization that most of the social ills that plague this country are by-products of a capitalist society. Racism was a necessary tool because the plantation owners needed a device to suppress bi-racial rebellions, like the Bacon Rebellion that Howard Zinn describes in his book, "A People's history of the United States," describing the mix and unity of disenfranchised whites and Black slaves. Racism was a necessary evil for capitalism to create divisions amongst groups that could possibly join forces and pose a threat to the power elite. Global warming, economic inequality, and poor education are all directly connected to capitalism. People have been asking me why I chose to join a socialist organization instead of a more Afrocentric organization. The answer is simple. Socialism gives power back to the people.

How Inmates Came to Join CCDS

By Alex Krehbiel

When I understood that capitalism was the cause of most problems in society and socialism was the solution, I became so passionate about wanting to share this knowledge that I talked about it every time I could. Being
in prison limited my opportunities, but there were times when we could
talk, like when we were out on the yard. When something even remotely
related to politics, economics, or philosophy was brought up around me,
I would interject a Marxist analysis into the discussion and when possible
end it by explaining how socialism would correct the injustices.

One time I did this when some people near me commented on Obama
opening up relations with Cuba and trying to get Congress to lift the
embargo. This discussion took place on the prison recreational yard. I
turned and joined them, even though I wasn't part of this group. I eased
myself into the conversation, listening first to what they were saying.
When I had a chance to speak I explained how the United States government had imposed an economic blockade against Cuba in an unceasing
effort to strangle or violently overthrow the Cuban government since
their 1959 revolution liberated the Cuban people from the capitalist dictatorship imposed by the US controlled Cuban puppet, Batista. I said
that if the embargo was lifted it would be good for the Cuban people and
Cuban socialism - a system designed to meet the needs of the people
and not one that allowed the wealthy elite to exploit others to enrich
themselves. They listened. A couple commented that what I said made
sense, but didn't say much more.

Most of my conversations went like that. Once a guy challenged me
over settler colonialism, repeating the standard government line that
colonized people willingly wanted to be part of the "commonwealth."
He railed against illegal immigrants and thought we needed a tougher
border patrol. I told him that to be factually correct we had to acknowledge that the colonial settlers from Europe were the original illegal immigrants and they committed genocide against the Native Americans,
killing most of therm. The Native Americans were hardly a group who
willingly joined the "commonwealth." He responded by saying that colonized people "lacked industriousness and ambition." That led our discussion to become more heated, with me almost shouting at him that
"evil is evil. There's no excuse for evil." Fortunately, inmates like that
are a rarity. People who are oppressed and who take the side of their
slave master present a sad picture.

"*From the Depths.*"

Most encounters were more friendly. In most cases I tried to point out in a cordial but forceful way the true history of the event under discussion. I soon earned a reputation as a "commie," an "obsessive socialist agitator," "that Black guy who's always badgering people about revolution, the need for class solidarity, and the unjustness of capitalism."

I realized I had to change my strategy. If I spoke about issues that directly impacted them I got a better reception. Then I would try to show how that issue or injustice was a result of capitalism. Some people listened, but most seemed resigned to the injustices because they felt the forces we were up against were too powerful to overthrow. After talking awhile I could see I was losing their attention, as they eyed the handball and basketball courts. While this did have a downside, it also had an upside: people knew I was serious and knowledgeable about politics, and about combating oppression and injustice, things that prison inmates are all too familiar with. In a sense it earned me some respect.

I tried to address the things they said. If someone said they didn't think anything could be changed, I spoke about the movements that were challenging corporate power in the US and other countries, like the labor movement, the Occupy Wall Street movement, Black Lives Matter movement, the climate justice movement, the Bernie Sanders campaign and many others, and pointed to past successful revolutions in Russia, Cuba and Vietnam to name just three that overthrew an old oppressive system and began building socialism. This got their attention. I met some guys who had read some books about these things, including Marxism, and they were more interested. I focused my attention on them. I wanted to find people who already knew something about the system and how and why it fostered injustice.

Importance of Marxist Literature

 One day when I was on the yard I was talking to a friend about some articles that we were looking at in a radical newspaper I had with me. I put the newspaper on a bench next to us and another guy picked it up while my friend and I continued talking. After a short time the guy on the bench entered our conversation saying he agreed with the articles in my paper and he wanted to know more. I shifted my attention to him and we talked. I learned that he had read some Marxism and agreed with it. We met on the yard many days after our initial meeting and had great discussions. I shared with him Marxist books and articles I was reading about fighting racism, police brutality and murders, and for social justice. He asked where I got these materials, how I learned this stuff and if I was involved with other people who believed the same things. He said he wanted to be a part of whatever I was involved with. I told him I was a member of Committees of Correspondence for Democracy and Socialism, and gave him some CCDS literature to read, including articles from The Mobilizer.

I met others who were interested in these topics and we began meeting on the yard for discussions. I would ask my parents to send me copies of books and articles for each of the guys in our study group so we read and discussed them when we met on the yard. The support and help I got from the outside was very helpful. Because CCDS has such a strong focus on the fight against racism and for the liberation of African Americans and other people of color, and on all the other social justice issues including the struggle for socialism, my friends were drawn to CCDS. Eventually I asked them if they wanted to join and five did join.

I learned several things doing this. It's important to stand up for what's just, and explain why. That meant educating myself, so I read voraciously. Then, the discussions I had with others led to an informal study group. A study or reading group allows for deeper study and discussion in an organized way, and when people do this work in a group they feel they are a part of something together. Another factor is that if you are talking to people who have suffered discrimination or oppression from the system, they will be more receptive. And people feel more trusting talking to someone like them. I also saw that if you want to win people to socialism and recruit them into a socialist organization you have to talk about socialism and that organization. There are other methods to help recruit members into CCDS, but that's what worked for us.

Police Reform or Community Control of the Police

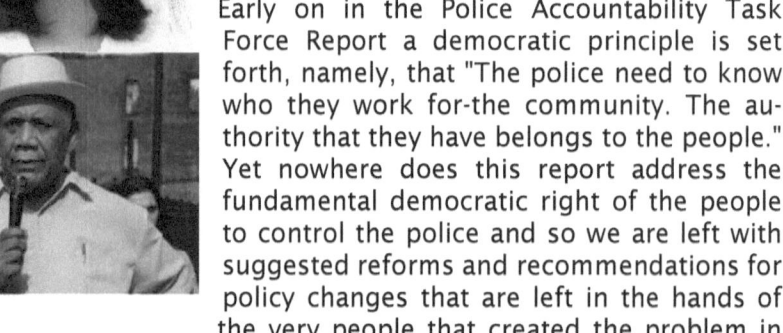

By Aislinn Pulley, Black Lives Matter Chicago and

Frank Chapman, Chicago Alliance against Racist & Political Repression

Early on in the Police Accountability Task Force Report a democratic principle is set forth, namely, that "The police need to know who they work for-the community. The authority that they have belongs to the people." Yet nowhere does this report address the fundamental democratic right of the people to control the police and so we are left with suggested reforms and recommendations for policy changes that are left in the hands of the very people that created the problem in the first place. If the police in fact worked for the community then we wouldn't be campaigning for community control of the police. The document itself is called: "POLICE ACCOUNTABILITY TASK FORCE RECOMMENDATIONS FOR REFORM: Restoring Trust between the Chicago Police and the Communities They Serve". The powers that be have been so poised, so prepared for a report such as this that they wasted no time in pumping it up in the media as a giant step forward in at least embarking on the long and torturous road of reform.

This is a long and detailed report that examines in detail particularity the institutionalized racist practices of the Chicago Police Department going back several decades, showing that the lack of accountability and the practice of excusing and justifying police crimes and misconduct is long standing. Also this Task Force declares at the outset that "The Police Accountability Task Force arose amidst a significant and historic public outcry. The outcry brought people into the streets, on social media and other venues to say in a very clear voice that they had reached a breaking point with the entire local law enforcement infrastructure. People were and are demanding accountability and real and lasting change. The outcry was not localized in any particular neighborhood or demographic, although communities of color and those ravaged by crime added some of the most poignant commentary."

Obviously the Black Lives Matter Movement and the broad based Black led peoples' movement for community control of the police (known in Chicago as CPAC) are the driving forces demanding police accountability. Therefore, we must approach this Task Force's report and recommendations from the standpoint of whether it contributes to the campaign for an all elected Civilian Police Accountability Council (CPAC), and how it furthers the demands of Black Lives Matter Chicago, Chicago Teachers Union, BYP100, Assata's Daughters, SEIU Locals 73 and SEIU HCII, Fight for 15, Trinity United Church of Christ, the Arab American Action Network, the Filipino Alliance, the Chicago Alliance Against Racist and Political Repression and others calling for justice now.

The Task Force report purports to be a response to the peoples' movement's demands for police accountability, but were that the case the Task Force would've recommended that all those complicit in the murder of Laquan McDonald be indicted and that Dante Servin be fired.

Justice now means first of all enacting the ordinance establishing community control of the police, CPAC. It also means:

"   Firing Dante Servin, the murderer of Rekia Boyd.

"   Firing and prosecuting the four police officers who lied in their reports to cover up the murder of Laquan McDonald.

"   Department of Justice prosecution of all police in Chicago who murdered and/or tortured people in violation of their federally protected
constitutional and human rights.

"   Mayor Rahm Emanuel must resign.

While we stand in agreement with many of the Task Force recommendations the fact is that the Task Force has no power to implement any of
them. In addition, there are still issues which are clearly not being addressed.

1. We agree that we arrived at this point of distrust in the police and
the criminal justice system because of racism and racist practices. However, it is clear that the police cannot self-correct this problem through
training. We must empower the people through CPAC to correct this
problem.

2. We agree that there is a need to address a mentality in the CPD that
the end justifies the means. Again we can't rely on the police and their
politician friends to self-correct this problem. The people must be em-
powered to hold the police accountable for their crimes and misconduct,
that is, the people who are presently powerless over the police must
have the power to tell the police how they want their communities po-
liced. CPAC will empower the people to write the rules with regard to
the use of deadly force, stop and frisk, and every other aspect of police
conduct.

3. Failure to make accountability a core value and imperative is a direct
result of the police policing themselves and placing themselves above
the law. They see accountability as an impediment. Being held accountable by the African American community and other communities of color
has thus far never even been considered. It is time to implement community control of the police.

4. The Task Force criticizes "Significant Underinvestment In Human Capital." What this means is that racism has been allowed to dictate who
polices our communities and how they police it. It means that from the
training academy to the streets that police are given the mentality that
they are to operate in our communities like an occupying army. There
should be an intolerance for racist attitudes at all levels but again this
problem cannot be solved internally. It will only be correctly approached
through community control of the police.

Basically this report is telling us that there are deep and abiding issues
such as massive unemployment, debilitating poverty, untreated mental

illness, drug addiction, etc., such conditions cause social unrest that in turn bring about mass protest, social rebellion, crime and mass incarceration. In our opinion the government's failure to address these issues causes disorder and the police as a para-military organization, is called upon to maintain order and quell social rebellion. Police crimes represent a direct threat to any hopes of us living in a fair and democratic society. Police repression is an ever present threat to all democratic struggles of the people and that is why we must fight for people power over police power.

No police Board! No IPRA! No Monitors, Auditors, or Overseers! Only Community Control of the Police! CPAC!!!!

Stop Violence against Women
and the LGBTQ Community

Editors' note: Violence against woman is at epidemic proportions and continues unabated. Too often it goes unpunished. In many cases it is condoned and encouraged by a culture of male supremacy and patriarchy. One-third of all women world-wide have been victims, according to several sources; other studies show the figure to be higher, and much higher for women of color and the LGBTQ community. The recent horrific mass murders at a gay nightclub in Orlando, Florida is the latest example of the latter.

When perpetrators of violence against woman are arrested, tried and convicted they too often are shown such leniency that it sends a message to other men that violence against women is okay. In many cases the woman is blamed and stigmatized, while the perpetrator is cast as the victim. The recent conviction of Stanford University student, Brock Turner, for raping an unconscious woman brought a sentence of just 6 months in jail, while his father pleaded to rescind the sentence that he claimed had ruined his son's life for just "20 minutes of action." No concern was expressed for ruining the woman's life. In addition to rape, beating, and murder, violence against women includes sexual harassment, coercion of women in any form, degrading women, treating women as inferior, and discriminating against women in any way.

We reprint here an address that Angela Davis gave at the Color of Violence Conference, held in Santa Cruz, California, October 10, 2000, which was published in Dialogue & Initiative in 2002.

The Color of Violence against Women

By Angela Davis

I feel extremely honored to have been invited to deliver this keynote address. This conference deserves to be called "historic" on many accounts. It is the first of its kind, and this is precisely the right intellectual season for such a gathering. The breadth and complexity of its concerns show the contradictions and possibilities of this historical moment. And just such a gathering can help us to imagine ways of attending to the ubiquitous violence in the lives of women of color that also radically subvert the institutions and discourses within which we are compelled by necessity to think and work.

I predict that this conference will be remembered as a milestone for feminist scholars and activists, marking a new moment in the history of anti-violence scholarship and organizing.

Many years ago when I was a student in San Diego, I was driving down the freeway with a friend when we encountered a black woman wandering along the shoulder. Her story was extremely disturbing. Despite her uncontrollable weeping, we were able to surmise that she had been raped and dumped along the side of the road. After a while, she was able to wave down a police car, thinking that they would help her. However, when the white policeman picked her up, he did not comfort her, but rather seized upon the opportunity to rape her once more.

I relate this story not for its sensational value, but for its metaphorical power.

Given the racist and patriarchal patterns of the state, it is difficult to envision the state as the holder of solutions to the problem of violence against women of color. However, as the anti-violence movement has been institutionalized and professionalized, the state plays an increasingly dominant role in how we conceptualize and create strategies to minimize violence against women. One of the major tasks of this conference, and of the anti-violence movement as a whole, is to address this contradiction, especially as it presents itself to poor communities of color.

The Advent of 'Domestic Violence'

Violence is one of those words that is a powerful ideological conductor, one whose meaning constantly mutates. Before we do anything else, we need to pay tribute to the activists and scholars whose ideological critiques made it possible to apply the category of domestic violence to those concealed layers of aggression systematically directed at women. These acts were for so long relegated to secrecy or, worse, considered normal.

Many of us now take for granted that misogynist violence is a legitimate political issue, but let us remember that a little more than two decades ago, most people considered "domestic violence" to be a private concern and thus not a proper subject of public discourse or political intervention. Only one generation separates us from that era of silence. The first speak-out against rape occurred in the early 1970s, and the first national organization against domestic violence was founded toward the end of that decade.

We have since come to recognize the epidemic proportions of violence within intimate relationships and the pervasiveness of date and acquaintance rape, as well as violence within and against same-sex intimacy. But we must also learn how to oppose the racist fixation on people of color as the primary perpetrators of violence, including domestic and sexual violence, and at the same time to fiercely challenge the real violence that men of color inflict on women. These are precisely the men who are already reviled as the major purveyors of violence in our society: the gang members, the drug-dealers, the drive-by shooters, the burglars, and assailants. In short, the criminal is figured as a black or Latino man who must be locked into prison.

One of the major questions facing this conference is how to develop an analysis that furthers neither the conservative project of sequestering millions of men of color in accordance with the contemporary dictates of globalized capital and its prison industrial complex, nor the equally conservative project of abandoning poor women of color to a continuum of violence that extends from the sweatshops through the prisons, to shelters, and into bedrooms at home.

How do we develop analyses and organizing strategies against violence against women that acknowledge the race of gender and the gender of race?

Women of Color on the Frontlines

Women of color have been active in the anti-violence movement since its beginnings. The first national organization addressing domestic violence was founded in 1978 when the United States Civil Rights Commission Consultation on Battered Women led to the founding of the National Coalition Against Domestic Violence. In 1980, the Washington, D.C. Rape Crisis Center sponsored the First National Conference on Third World Women and Violence.

The following year a Women of Color Task Force was created within the National Coalition Against Domestic Violence. To make some historical connections, it is significant that the U.S. Third World Women's Caucus formed that same year within the National Women Studies Association, and the groundbreaking book This Bridge Called My Back was first published.

Many of these activists have helped to develop a more complex understanding about the overlapping, cross-cutting, and often contradictory relationships among race, class, gender, and sexuality that militate against a simplistic theory of privatized violence in women's lives. Clearly, the powerful slogan first initiated by the feminist movement--"the personal is political"--is far more complicated than it initially appeared to be.

The early feminist argument that violence against women is not inherently a private matter, but has been privatized by the sexist structures of the state, the economy, and the family has had a powerful impact on public consciousness.

Yet, the effort to incorporate an analysis that does not reify gender has not been so successful. The argument that sexual and domestic violence is the structural foundation of male dominance sometimes leads to a hierarchical notion that genital mutilation in Africa and sati, or wife-burning, in India are the most dreadful and extreme forms of the same violence against women which can be discovered in less appalling manifestations in Western cultures.

Other analyses emphasize a greater incidence of misogynist violence in poor communities and communities of color, without necessarily acknowledging the greater extent of police surveillance in these communities--directly and through social service agencies. In other words, precisely because the primary strategies for addressing violence against women rely on the state and on constructing gendered assaults on women as "crimes," the criminalization process further bolsters the racism of the courts and prisons. Those institutions, in turn, further contribute to violence against women.

On the one hand, we should applaud the courageous efforts of the many activists who are responsible for a new popular consciousness of violence against women, for a range of legal remedies, and for a network of shelters, crisis centers, and other sites where survivors are able to find support. But on the other hand, uncritical reliance on the government has resulted in serious problems. I suggest that we focus our thinking on this contradiction: Can a state that is thoroughly infused with racism, male dominance, class-bias, and homophobia and that constructs itself in and through violence act to minimize violence in the lives of women? Should we rely on the state as the answer to the problem of violence against women?

The soon-to-be-released video by Nicole Cusino (assisted by Ruth Gilmore) on California prison expansion and its economic impact on rural and urban communities includes a poignant scene in which Vanessa Gomez describes how the deployment of police and court anti-violence strategies put her husband away under the Three Strikes law. She describes a verbal altercation between herself and her husband, who was angry with her for not cutting up liver for their dog's meal, since, she said, it was her turn to cut the liver.

According to her account, she insisted that she would prepare the dog's food, but he said no, he was already doing it. She says that she grabbed him and, in trying to take the knife away from him, seriously cut her fingers. In the hospital, the incident was reported to the police. Despite the fact that Ms. Gomez contested the prosecutor's version of the events, her husband was convicted of assault. Because of two previous convictions as a juvenile, he received a sentence under California's Three Strikes law of 25 years to life, which he is currently serving.

I relate this incident because it so plainly shows the facility with which the state can assimilate our opposition to gender domination into projects of racial--which also means gender--domination.

Militarized Violence

Gina Dent has observed that one of the most important accomplishments of this conference is to foreground Native American women within the category "women of color." As Kimberle Crenshaw's germinal study on violence against women suggests, the situation of Native American women shows that we must also include within our analytical framework the persisting colonial domination of indigenous nations and national formations within and outside the presumed territorial boundaries of the U.S. The U.S. colonial state's racist, sexist, and homophobic brutality in dealing with Native Americans once again shows the futility of relying upon the juridical or legislative processes of the state to resolve these problems.

How then can one expect the state to solve the problem of violence against women, when it constantly recapitulates its own history of colonialism, racism, and war? How can we ask the state to intervene when, in fact, its armed forces have always practiced rape and battery against "enemy" women? In fact, sexual and intimate violence against women has been a central military tactic of war and domination.

Yet the approach of the neoliberal state is to incorporate women into these agencies of violence--to integrate the armed forces and the police.

How do we deal with the police killing of Amadou Diallo, whose wallet was putatively misapprehended as a gun--or Tanya Haggerty in Chicago, whose cell phone was the potential weapon that allowed police to justify her killing? By hiring more women as police officers? Does the argument that women are victimized by violence render them inefficient agents of violence? Does giving women greater access to official violence help to minimize informal violence?

Even if this were the case, would we want to embrace this as a solution? Are women essentially immune from the forms of adaptation to violence that are so foundational to police and military culture?

Carol Burke, a civilian teaching in the U.S. Naval Academy, argues that "sadomasochistic cadence calls have increased since women entered the brigade of midshipmen in 1976." She quotes military songs that are so cruelly pornographic that I would feel uncomfortable quoting them in public, but let me give one comparatively less offensive example:

The ugliest girl I ever did see
Was beatin' her face against a tree
I picked her up; I punched her twice.
She said, "Oh Middy, you're much too nice.

If we concede that something about the training structures and the operations they are expected to carry out makes the men (and perhaps also women) in these institutions more likely to engage in violence within their intimate relationships, why then is it so difficult to develop an analysis of violence against women that takes the violence of the state into account?

The major strategy relied on by the women's anti-violence movement of criminalizing violence against women will not put an end to violence against women--just as imprisonment has not put an end to "crime" in general.

I should say that this is one of the most vexing issues confronting feminists today. On the one hand, it is necessary to create legal remedies for women who are survivors of violence. But on the other hand, when the remedies rely on punishment within institutions that further promote violence--against women and men, how do we work with this contradiction?

How do we avoid the assumption that previously "private" modes of violence can only be rendered public within the context of the state's apparatus of violence?

The Crime Bill

It is significant that the 1994 Violence Against Women Act was passed by Congress as Title IV of the Violent Crime Control and Law Enforcement Act of 1994--the Crime Bill. This bill attempted to address violence against women within domestic contexts, but at the same time it facilitated the incarceration of more women--through Three Strikes and other provisions. The growth of police forces provided for by the Crime Bill will certainly increase the numbers of people subject to the brutality of police violence.

Prisons are violent institutions. Like the military, they render women vulnerable in an even more systematic way to the forms of violence they may have experienced in their homes and in their communities. Women's prison experiences point to a continuum of violence at the intersection of racism, patriarchy, and state power.

A Human Rights Watch report entitled "All Too Familiar: Sexual Abuse of Women in U.S. Prisons" says: "Our findings indicate that being a woman prisoner in U.S. state prisons can be a terrifying experience. If you are sexually abused, you cannot escape from your abuser. Grievance or investigatory procedures, where they exist, are often ineffectual, and correctional employees continue to engage in abuse because they believe they will rarely be held accountable, administratively or criminally. Few people outside the prison walls know what is going on or care if they do know. Fewer still do anything to address the problem."

Recently, 31 women filed a class action law suit against the Michigan Department of Corrections, charging that the department failed to prevent sexual violence and abuse by guards and civilian staff. These women have been subjected to serious retaliations, including being raped again!

At Valley State Prison in California, the chief medical officer told Ted Koppel on national television that he and his staff routinely subjected women to pelvic examinations, even if they just had colds. He explained that these women have been imprisoned for a long time and have no male contact, and so they actually enjoy these pelvic examinations. Koppel sent the tape of this interview to the prison and he was eventually dismissed. According to the Department of Corrections, he will never be allowed to have contact with patients again. But this is just the tip of the iceberg. The fact that he felt able to say this on national television gives you a sense of the horrendous conditions in women's prisons.

There are no easy solutions to all the issues I have raised and that so many of you are working on. But what is clear is that we need to come together to work toward a far more nuanced framework and strategy than the anti-violence movement has ever yet been able to elaborate.

We want to continue to contest the neglect of domestic violence against women, the tendency to dismiss it as a private matter. We need to develop an approach that relies on political mobilization rather than legal remedies or social service delivery. We need to fight for temporary and long-term solutions to violence and simultaneously think about and link global capitalism, global colonialism, racism, and patriarchy--all the forces that shape violence against women of color. Can we, for example, link a strong demand for remedies for women of color who are targets of rape and domestic violence with a strategy that calls for the abolition of the prison system?

I conclude by asking you to support the new organization initiated by Andrea Smith, the organizer of this conference. Such an organization contesting violence against women of color is especially needed to connect, advance, and organize our analytic and organizing efforts. Hopefully this organization will act as a catalyst to keep us thinking and moving together in the future.

Angela Davis is a professor, scholar, activist and a founding member of the CCDS.

LGBTQ Staff at 350.org
Decry Orlando Killings

Editors' Note: The killing of 50 people and wounding 53 more at a gay nightclub in Orlando, Florida prompted mass protests and vigils across the country, and a 24-hour sit-in by Democrats in Congress demanding gun control legislation that is being blocked by Republicans. We reprint here a statement written by LBGTQ staff members at the environmental organization, 350.org.

We write this with tears in our eyes. We haven't been able to get them out of our eyes since waking up on Sunday morning and seeing the news about the massacre in Orlando, Florida.

To be honest, we've been hesitant to write this. The reality of backlash, from individual emails to anger from governments and our own communities, is real and quite scary. Knowing this, we still chose to write this statement, because it's important and needs to be said.

You might be asking yourself, why is an organization who focuses on climate change, responding to this horrifying night. Because we're all connected, as is our fight.

As LGBTQ+ staff at 350, we are a part of this movement, we are connected to this movement, and our survival depends on this movement for climate justice.

There are many folks at 350.org, in our networks, at our actions, in our community that identify as LGBTQ+. There are many of us who see the intersections of our race, class, gender and sexual orientation as inextricably linked to the fight against fossil fuels and for our climate.

And to be honest, intersectionality is complicated. At the heart of it, we live complicated lives, with overlapping identities. Many of us who are shoulder to shoulder with you in the streets are LGBTQ+. Many of us who've fought alongside you to stop climate change, and to ensure communities have clean air and water, are LGBTQ+. Some of us are also Latinx, as were those targeted in Orlando. And some of us are also Muslim, and are already facing a different sort of backlash as a result of this attack. What we need is to be able to bring our whole selves in this movement, which means being clear about what we need when our LGBTQ+ lives and bodies are under attack.

To those of you who identify as LGBTQ+, we see you, we stand with you, and we love you. We know that you're our neighbors, and that our arms are linked with yours in the streets. We know that you're our family, and our colleagues. We know that some of you are still hiding this part of yourselves, and we know what that feels like. We love you.

For those of you who aren't part of this community, take this time to reflect on those in your life who are LGBTQ+. Please reach out to them. Let them know they're loved and are seen. We don't need you to know the right words. We need you to tell us that you love us. For us to come together as a movement, and fight for a just future together, we need to know that you're here with us.

This week is tough for many of us. To get through this, we need to let people know where we stand. Our organization fights for a just future. That doesn't mean only climate justice, it means justice across all fronts. If we aren't fighting for a future that is safe for everyone, then what are we truly fighting for?

Let us make sure to lift up those who will undoubtedly be targeted as a response to this attack. Not just the LGBTQ community, but also folks who are Arab, Muslim, and the community targeted by this attack- the Latinx community. We uplift our siblings who hold many of these identities, and we see you. We love you.

If we are to move forward together in all of our interconnected struggles, we must make sure that everyone is cared for and safe. We cannot fight the biggest issue impacting our world without everyone. We cannot fight climate change without standing with each other when we come under attack.

350.org stands in solidarity with the communities affected by the homophobic attack in Orlando. We grieve for those who were slain, and we stand in solidarity with the communities who are struggling to heal and survive. And we will not let our grief and fear turn to hatred.

If you're able to make a financial contribution to help the victims of the Orlando shooting, here's where you can do so:

· Equality Florida's GoFundMe Campaign: donate to the families affected by the shooting.

·   Southerners on New Ground: Queer Liberation organization made up of LGBTQ people of color, immigrants, and other marginalized communities in the South (US).

·   The Muslim Alliance for Sexual and Gender Diversity: An organization that is focused on connecting and empowering LGBTQ Muslims.

·   The Center Orlando's GoFundMe Campaign: providing a crisis services in the Orlando area and raising money for the affected families;

With so much heartbreak, and so much love,

Your friends at 350.org and our LGBTQ staff, including:

Linda Capato Jr
Elliot Altomare
Sabelo Narasimhan
Betamia Coronel
Everette R.H. Thompson
Vanessa Arcara
Emma Youfrau
Ellen Gibson
Liangyi Chang
Dani Heffernan
Kendall Mackey
Louise Hazan

Reference

http://350.org/orlando/?akid=14267.9757.snHdZV&rd=1&t=1&utm_medium=email

Labor on the March

Editor's Note: We begin this section with a photo essay by David Bacon on cross-border labor solidarity between Mexican and US workers. He gives special attention in this essay to the rich history of the struggles of Mexican workers for justice, a story we rarely see in the US mass media.

20 Years of Cross-Border Solidarity

A History in Photographs

By David Bacon
NACLA Report on the Americas, May 2016

Unions and social movements face a basic question on both sides of the Mexico/U.S. border - can they win the battles they face today, especially political ones, without joining their efforts together? Fortunately, this is not an abstract question. Struggles have taken place in maquiladoras for two decades all along the border. Many centers and collectives of workers have come together over those years. Walkouts over unpaid wages, or indemnización, as well as terrible working conditions are still common.

What's more, local activists still find ways to support these actions through groups like the Collective Ollin Calli in Tijuana and its network of allies across the border in Tijuana, the San Diego Maquiladora Workers Solidarity Network. Other forms of solidarity have been developed through groups like the Comité Fronterizo de Obreras and the Coalition for Justice in the Maquiladoras. And long-term relations have been created between unions like the United Electrical Workers and the Authentic

Labor Front, and the United Steel Workers and the Mexican Mineros. More recently, binational support networks have formed for farm workers in Baja California, and workers are actively forming new networks of resistance and solidarity in the plantons outside factories in Ciudad Juárez.

Over the years, support from many U.S. unions and churches, and from unions and labor institutions in Mexico City, has often been critical in helping these collectives survive, especially during the pitched battles to win legal status for independent unions. At other moments, however, the worker groups in the maquiladoras and the cities of the border have had to survive on their own, or with extremely limited resources.

These photographs show both the conditions people on the border are trying to change, and some of the efforts they've made to change them, in cooperation with groups in the U.S. There have been many such efforts - this is just a look at some.

TIJUANA BAJA CALIFORNIA NORTE, MEXICO - 1993 - Workers vote in a union election outside the Tijuana maquiladora of Plásticos Bajacal. Voting is public, and workers have to declare aloud whether they're voting for the company union or their own independent union. Lic. Mandujano, head of the labor board in Tijuana and an ally of the companies and the company unions, points to a worker and demands that he declare which union he's voting for, as company officials look on, along with Carmen Valadez, a representative of the independent union. The maquiladora organizing drive at Plásticos Bajacal in 1993 first highlighted for U.S.

unions the reality of public union representation elections and the lack of the secret ballot. The San Diego Support Committee for Maquiladora Workers raised enough money to pay lost time for fired workers, so they could continue organizing the factory.

TIJUANA BAJA CALIFORNIA NORTE, MEXICO - 1995 - Women workers from the National O-Ring maquiladora demonstrate for women's rights during the May Day parade in Tijuana. Their factory was closed, and the women were laid off and blacklisted, after they filed charges of sexual harassment against their employer. The plant manager had organized a "beauty contest" at a company picnic, and ordered women workers to parade in bikinis. Supported by the San Diego Support Committee for Maquiladora Workers, women filed suit in a U.S. Federal court, which surprisingly accepted jurisdiction. The company then gave women severance pay for the loss of their jobs.

LÁZARO CÁRDENAS, MICHOACÁN, MEXICO - 1995 - As the Mexican government moved to privatize the ports along the Pacific coast, the International Longshore and Warehouse Union sent a delegation to talk with Mexican dockworkers and their union. In Lázaro Cárdenas workers had a long history of insurgent unionism in the Sicartsa steel mill. Some later came to Los Angeles, where they organized among immigrant workers there. In the port, workers tried to preserve their contract and wages, and U.S. dockworkers offered to support them.

TIJUANA BAJA CALIFORNIA NORTE, MEXICO - 1997 - Workers vote for an independent union in the first union election at Han Young, an auto parts manufacturing company Workers are voting by open ballot in the office of the state labor board. Surrounding them are Benedicto Martinez, general secretary of the Authentic Workers Front, and activists from the San Diego Support Committee for Maquiladora Workers, including videographer Fred Lonidier.

TORREÓN, COAHUILA, MEXICO -
2002 - When the wave of murders of
young women began in Ciu-
dad Juárez, activists on both
sides of the border organized
demonstrations to make the
crisis a public political issue.
In Torreón, one organization
of the mothers of disappeared
women, "Nuestras Hijas de Re-
greso a la Casa," organized a
march with the Coalition for
Justice in the Maquiladoras.
Fermina, a mother of one of
the women murdered and disappeared in Juárez, marched
with other mothers to call on
Mexican authorities to investi-
gate the cases.

MATAMOROS, COAHUILA, MEXICO - 2006 - Supporters of APPO (Asam-
blea Popular de los Pueblos de Oaxaca -- the Popular Assembly of Oaxacan People) demonstrated at the US-Mexico border crossing in Matamoros during the teachers' strike and subsequent insurrection in Oaxaca.

The demonstrators called for the resignation of Governor Ulises Ruiz and demanded that the Mexican government withdraw federal forces from that state. Martha Ojeda, director of the Coalition for Justice in the Maquiladoras, was an organizer of the demonstration, and Rosemary Hennesey, a teacher at Rice University, carried a sign announcing support for the teachers by the Kansas City Cross Border Network.

NUEVO LAREDO, TAMAULIPAS, MEXICO - 2009 - The settlement of Blanca Navidad, on the outskirts of Nuevo Laredo, just south of the U.S. border. Blanca Navidad was created by workers looking for land to build a place to live. It is part of a network of radical communities on the border, and throughout Mexico, sympathetic with the Zapatista movement. Most residents work in the maquiladoras. When the community came under attack by state authorities, who threatened to bulldoze their homes, activists came from Texas to defend it.

MEXICO CITY, DF, MEXICO - 2010 - A striking teacher from Michoacán demonstrates on the Reforma, in front of a line of police. Teachers came from states where the National Coordinating Committee of Education Workers (CNTE), the leftwing organization within the Mexican teachers' union, leads the teachers' organization. They protested proposals by the Mexican government to reform the educational system by introducing standardized testing and removing job protections for teachers. U.S. and Canadian teachers have supported their efforts to defeat these proposals, which have come from U.S. AID and private foundations promoting corporate education reform. Together they've organized a TriNational Coalition to Defend Public Education.

MEXICO CITY, DF, MEXICO - 2011 - Trade union activists and other popular organizations protest in Mexico City's main square, the Zócalo, on the day Mexican President Felipe Calderón gave his annual speech about the state of the country. The protest, called the Day of the Indignant, was organized by unions including the Mexican Electrical Workers (SME) because the Mexican government fired 44,000 electrical workers and dissolved the state-owned company they worked for, in an effort to smash their union. Protestors also demanded jobs, labor rights, and an end to the repression of political dissidents. SME members had been camped out in the square, and several mounted a months-long hunger strike. Many U.S. activists came to the protest and visited the encampment during the hunger strike.

MEXICO CITY, DF, MEXICO - 2014 - Members of the National Coordinating Committee of Education Workers (CNTE) and the Mexican Electrical Workers Union (SME) marched with U.S. and Canadian labor activists to Mexico City's main square, the Zócalo, on the 20th anniversary of the implementation of the North American Free Trade Agreement. The marchers protested the educational, economic, and political reforms passed over the last year by the Mexican government and the ruling Party of the Institutionalized Revolution. These reforms set the stage for the privatization of the oil and electrical industry, the implementation of corporate education reform and social benefit policies, and changes to the country's labor law. Activists also protested the negotiation of a new trade agreement, the Trans-Pacific Partnership.

TIJUANA, BAJA CALIFORNIA NORTE, MEXICO - 2015 - Striking farm workers from the San Quintin Valley marched to the U.S.-Mexico border to draw attention to the fact that the tomatoes and strawberries they pick are exported to the U.S. The workers are almost all indigenous Mixtec and Triqui migrants from Oaxaca, in southern Mexico. At the border they were met by delegations of activists, who rallied on the other side in support.

BURLINGTON, WA - 2015 - Farm workers and their supporters march to the office of Sakuma Farms, a large berry grower, where they went on strike in 2013. The workers are demanding that the company bargain a contract with their union, Familias Unidas por la Justicia. They organized a boycott of Driscoll's, the giant berry distributor, accusing it of being responsible for the violation of their labor rights at Sakuma, since the company buys all the Sakuma blueberries the workers pick. The workers are indigenous migrants from Oaxaca. They also demonstrated in support of the indigenous Oaxacan farm workers in Baja California, who were on strike against growers who also distribute their berries through Driscoll's.

SAN FRANCISCO, CA - 2015 - Two students of the Ayotzinapa teachers training school in Guerrero, Mexico, and the parents of two others, marched with supporters in San Francisco to protest the disappearance of 43 students from the school in September 2014, and the murder by the Mexican police of three others. The four individuals were part of three caravans traveling simultaneously through U.S. cities to publicize the cases.

References

WORKING HANDS
Photographs of Longshoremen by Frank Silva
Photographs of Farm and Recycling Workers by David Bacon

Photocentral Gallery
1099 E St.
Hayward, CA
6/4 to 8/6/16
Reception: Saturday, June 4, 2-5PM

ON THE STREETS : UNDER THE TREES
Homelessness and the struggle for housing

in urban and rural California
Photographs by David Bacon

Asian Resource Gallery
317 Ninth St at Harrison
Oakland, CA
May - June, 2016
Reception: Tuesday, May 24, 6PM

In the 38th Greater Bay Area Journalism Awards David Bacon won first-place in the photo series category for his August 6, 2014 cover story for the East Bay Express, "Living on the Streets of Oakland," a photo essay that examined the situation of homeless people in the Bay Area's third largest city.

THE REALITY CHECK - David Bacon blog
http://davidbaconrealitycheck.blogspot.com

EN LOS CAMPOS DEL NORTE: Farm worker photographs on the U.S./Mexico border wall

http://us7.campaign-archive2.com/?u=fc67a76dbb9c31aaee896aff7&id=0644c65ae5&e=dde0321ee7

Youtube interview about the show with Alfonso Caraveo (Spanish)

https://www.youtube.com/watch?v=lJeE1NO4c_M&feature=youtu.be

David Bacon radio review of the movie, Cesar Chavez
https://soundcloud.com/kpfa-fm-94-1-berkeley/upfronts-david-bacon-reviews-film-on-cesar-chavez-and-the-grape-strike

Interviews with David Bacon about his book, The Right to Stay Home:

Book TV: A presentation of the ideas in The Right to Stay Home at the CUNY Graduate Center
http://booktv.org/Watch/14961/The+Right+to+Stay+Home+How+US+Policy+Drives+Mexican+Migration.aspx

KPFK - Uprisings with Sonali Kohatkar
http://uprisingradio.org/home/2013/09/27/the-right-to-stay-home-how-us-policy-drives-mexican-migration/

KPFA - Upfront with Brian Edwards Tiekert
https://soundcloud.com/kpfa-fm-94-1-berkeley/david-bacon-on-up-
front-9-20

Books by David Bacon

The Right to Stay Home: How US Policy Drives Mexican Migration (Beacon Press, 2013)

http://www.beacon.org/productdetails.cfm?PC=2328

Illegal People -- How Globalization Creates Migration and Criminalizes
Immigrants (Beacon Press, 2008)

Recipient: C.L.R. James Award, best book of 2007-2008
http://www.beacon.org/Illegal-People-P780.aspx

Communities Without Borders (Cornell University/ILR Press, 2006)

http://www.cornellpress.cornell.edu/book/?GCOI=80140100558350

The Children of NAFTA, Labor Wars on the U.S./Mexico Border (University of California, 2004)
http://www.ucpress.edu/books/pages/9989.html

En Español:

EL DERECHO A QUEDARSE EN CASA (Critica - Planeta de Libros)
http://www.planetadelibros.com.mx/el-derecho-a-quedarse-en-casa-
libro-205607.html

HIJOS DE LIBRE COMERCIA (El Viejo Topo)
http://www.tienda.elviejotopo.com/prestashop/capitalismo/1080-
hijos-del-libre-comercio-deslocalizaciones-y-precariedad-
9788496356368.html?search_query=david+bacon&results=1

http://davidbaconrealitycheck.blogspot.com/2016/05/twenty-years-of-
cross-border-solidarity.html

http://www.tandfonline.com/doi/full/10.1080/10714839.2016.11703
01

For more articles and images, see http://dbacon.igc.org

Key to Labor's Rising: Uniting With Justice Movements and the Left

By Paul Krehbiel

Paul Krehbiel
Teamsters, 1984.

When worker's struggles to protect and improve their wages and benefits unite with community coalitions and left and Marxist politics a force is created that can change society. After 40 years of intense attacks by corporations and countless losses for working people, it sounds like pie-in-the-sky. But it's happening. Growing numbers of workers and unions are taking a stand, fighting to defend and improve their working and living conditions, working with movements fighting for social justice, opposing racism and sexism, violence against people of color, women and the LBGTQ community, fighting for climate justice, and against war. The left is playing an important role in this social justice labor activism.

It's not happening evenly nor everywhere, and it's still in its early stages in some places. In other places this dynamic is stronger than others. But when it happens (like the recent victories in the $15 an hour minimum wage movement), victories are won that wouldn't have been achieved earlier. When it happens on a big scale big victories transform the relationship between capitalists and workers, putting labor and the people's movements on higher political ground and weakening capital. (The best examples are the victories of the 1930's and 1940's that empowered and organized millions of workers into unions, dealt a blow against racism, and won the New Deal which improved life for most of society.) Many small victories pave the way for larger ones. Lacking any of these elements diminishes the outcome.

All of these elements and forces are alive today and growing. Workers are fighting in many industries to protect and advance their working and living conditions. Low wage workers in fast food, Wal-Mart and other industries and their allies have linked up with social justice movements, such as Black Lives Matter and the Moral Mondays, to name just two, to maximize the strength of both movements. Fast food workers are aided by the Service Employees International Union, and Wal-Mart workers by the United Food and Commercial Workers. Unionization is one important goal. Many of the low paid workers movements are led by young African-American, Latino, Asian-Pacific Islander, Arab-American and white workers, creating a strong multi-racial movement that has largely won the ideological battle for a $15 minimum wage. They are becoming a part of the most multi-racial social movement in the country, the labor movement. This was not on anyone's radar screen several years ago. But the potential for greater victories are large, with 3.5 million unorganized fast food workers and 1.4 million Wal-Mart workers in the United States.

Other organizing campaigns are underway in a wide range of industries across the country, from the Auto Workers union campaigns, especially in Mississippi and other southern states (led by African-American workers in many locations), to teaching assistants and adjunct professors nearly everywhere. Union workers are resisting company demands for crippling give-backs in major industries from coast to coast. Some 40,000 Verizon workers centered in the northeast, members of the Communications Workers of America and the International Brotherhood of Electrical Workers, are striking to save their jobs. Nurses in the National Nurses Union are striking in three states to protect their health insurance and other benefits. Teamsters are fighting to protect their pensions, while honoring other union's picket-lines. Growing numbers of workers in most industries see the relentless corporate attacks as inherent in the capitalist system and will continue unless some fundamental changes take place.

The Fight for $15

How did the Fight for $15 gain such widespread support? First, it's very difficult to live on the national minimum wage, $7.25 an hour, so low wage workers have a personal incentive to act. While some states have raised the minimum wage slightly, it still isn't enough. The objective conditions are ripe for change. Now there needed to be a catalyst.

Low income workers, first in New York City, waged strikes and rallies for $15 an hour and a union. These protests spread across the country, dramatizing worker's grievances and garnering public support. This pressure led a growing number of cities to pass a $15 an hour minimum wage law.

The left played a role early on. Leftists among the workers and in the labor movement helped spark and organize the initial movement. Community and political campaigns, often initiated by leftists, helped. One of the earliest was led by Socialist Alternative Seattle Council candidate Kshama Sawant. Her Marxist analysis, correct reading of the mood of Seattle voters, and bold promotion of a social justice agenda generated a groundswell of support for a $15 minimum wage. This movement helped elect her to the Seattle City Council where she and the larger movement campaigned to win majority support of the City Council to pass the $15 minimum wage for the city of Seattle. This victory set an example for other cities across the country, and other cities and two states (New York and California) have passed a $15 minimum wage for certain classifications of workers, in most cases rising incrementally to $15 over several years.

As this battle unfolded, presidential candidate, Bernie Sanders, a democratic socialist running for the Democratic Party nomination, raised the demand for a $15 minimum wage along with a very progressive program to end skyrocketing income inequality, break up Wall Street banks, create 13 million jobs rebuilding our country's infrastructure, stop billionaires from buying elections, provide free public college education, establish improved Medicare-for-All, and much more. His demand for a $15 minimum wage reached many millions of people everywhere and was welcomed by strong public support. By the end of the primary season, Bernie Sanders had received over 12 million votes, won primaries and caucuses in 23 states, and made the fight for a $15 minimum wage a just demand in the eyes of tens of millions of people from coast to coast. Bernie Sanders also made it acceptable to publicly talk about and advocate socialism after 65 years of the establishment successfully denouncing it, and half or more of the population now look favorably upon it.   This new development should not be underestimated. It has opened doors for the left in the labor movement and among many other constituencies. Socialist ideas will help build a stronger labor movement and people's organizations, and stronger socialist movements and organizations.

Dealing with Contradictions

While the fight for $15 continues to win new supporters, there are some wrinkles in the campaign that could hold it back. One is that the union supporting the low income workers who are demanding $15, Service Employees International Union (SEIU), is backing Hillary Clinton for president, who is supporting only a $12 an hour minimum wage.

Of course, organizations decide to endorse candidates based on more than the candidate's position on one issue. But in the 2016 presidential race, Bernie Sanders has by far the best record and platform on all issues of importance to working people and society as a whole, and most unions know it. A number of unions endorsed him, but the majority did not. They instead opted to support Hillary Clinton, despite her uneven record on labor which included support for anti-labor bills such as job-killing free trade agreements. After 40 years of getting kicked in the teeth by big corporations and corporate politicians, how could most unions fail to support the best and only candidate committed to fighting for unions and working people?

While answers vary from one union to another, several common rationales emerge. One of the most prevalent is that most union leaders have had a working relationship with the leadership of the Democratic Party going back to President Roosevelt when his New Deal of the 1930's greatly helped the working-class and its unions. While those days are long in the past, many union leaders don't want to risk hurting that relationship by refusing to back the Democratic Party's establishment's choice.

Role of Democrats

Even though the Democratic Party has failed to help labor on many of the most crucial issues for years (such as getting card check to help more workers join unions, as one of many issues), most union leaders felt keeping ties with the Democratic Party is some help in blunting the attack of the much more anti-labor, anti-people Republicans. Growing numbers of people know that the top leaders of the Democratic Party are owners of or have strong ties to many of the largest corporations and banks, the same corporations that Bernie Sanders has exposed and condemned. These corporate connections are worse and more right-wing in the Republican Party. At the base of the Democratic Party are millions of workers, people of color, progressives and socialists who are in a struggle with the corporate leaders who dominate the party nationally. Class struggle is going on in both major political parties, though it is unknown yet how it will play out in either one.

Marxists in the labor movement, and even some non-Marxist progressives, understand that a political party run by major corporate owners must be challenged when that party supports issues that harm workers and the general public. While continuing to support Bernie Sanders, most of us know that defeating Donald Trump and other Republicans will mean supporting Democratic Party candidates in most races. But that doesn't stop us from calling out the Democrats when they support anti-labor and anti-people policies, and supporting leftist third party candidates when they won't play a spoiler role that helps elect Republicans.

Developing a Winning Strategy

During World War II, labor across the board, from Communists to con-servatives, united with the Roosevelt's Democratic Party to fight Hitler and the spread of fascism. After fascism was defeated, the Republican and Democratic Party leaders and employers turned against the left in labor to split especially the left leadership from the rest of the union. Corporate strategy was to whip up fear among workers and the general public against socialism, communism, and the Soviet Union by waging a massive 15 year campaign against some real but mostly made-up short-comings and errors of the US left. Lies, smears, threats, firings, black-listing and other forms of repression were the weapons of capitalism.
That corporate campaign was largely successful and it greatly weakened the labor movement. Slowly, the left has rebuilt some of its strength in the labor movement (though nowhere near what it was in the 1930's), and that has led to more progressive and even left leaders getting elect-ed in some unions. But there is still considerable resistance and a hold-over to conservative ideologies and fear from the past.

Not surprisingly, the unions which are led by leaders who are more con-sciously left in their ideology are the unions that endorsed Bernie Sand-ers. A number of union leaders know that the constant attacks on work-ers and our unions are due to the normal functioning of the capitalist economic system, not simply because of some bad individuals in corpo-rate board rooms. But labor's solutions vary. Some believe that reforms can be won to reign in the worst abuses of capitalism. Some believe that the ultimate solution has to be socialism, a system where goods and services are produced to meet the needs of the people, not create huge private profits to enrich a relatively small group of very wealthy business owners. Some believe in both, and advocate fighting for reforms today that lay the foundation for transforming society to socialism.

Our job in the union movement is to work with all union leaders and rank-and-file members who want to fight the cutbacks and abuses, and to expand democracy and empower workers. In the course of that strug-gle we will win growing numbers to the political left, and to socialism and Marxism. Building the Marxist left is important because Marx, more than any other thinker, best uncovered and explained the essence of capitalist exploitation and oppression. But it will take a plan. Simply handing out a socialist paper will not suffice. We have to work with labor on issues workers and unions feel are important, and on issues that we feel are important, in a way that helps union members see the connections between what they believe today and the next step on the path to the left. Our goal is to move the entire political spectrum to the left, helping to develop leaders along the way, including Marxist leaders. History and recent struggles point the way.

Marxist Analysis is Key

In unions where leftists and Marxists are active and work in a smart way, the chances for better outcomes increases. Here's one fairly recent example. I was with a Service Employees International Union (SEIU) local union representing public service workers in Los Angeles in the late 1990's and 2000's. The members wanted a union that would fight harder to protect the members' interests, and a group of workers campaigned for change. There were progressives, leftists of various beliefs, Marxists, and non-political people involved in a reform effort. The group supported a militant worker to run for president of the local union. This worker decried the abuses of management and had a strong fighting spirit and commitment to change the union. He wasn't a Marxist, but most supporters felt that he had enough of what it would take to fight management abuses and win improvements. He was elected president of the local and things went along well for a while.

But, then the union faced a big shortfall in the government budget in 2002 and management wanted to terminate thousands of workers and close neighborhood health clinics and two of the county's six public hospitals in response to the shortfall in funds. The local union president said that nothing could be done, there just wasn't enough money. The leftists and especially the Marxists said that there was a different solution. We urged the union leaders to wage a campaign to stop all the layoffs and cuts, and a public campaign to raise the taxes slightly on the wealthy to a previous level to make up the shortfall. The local union president reiterated his earlier position. He said the union should not rock the boat with management, echoing the views of Andy Stern, then national president of SEIU, and hope the cutbacks wouldn't be too severe. "We don't have a choice," the local union president said. "We have to get into bed with management." The union's General Manager said we had to get used to a smaller Los Angeles County Department of Health Services.

The progressives in the union and especially the Marxists disagreed. Among the Marxists were leaders and members of the staff union, and they did research and found that there was a lot of money in Los Angeles County and beyond, and with other leftists took the lead to educate and agitate for a public campaign to raise revenue to make up the shortfall. The union leaders ignored these efforts, and county management cut most of the county health clinics. The union leaders remained silent. But, as the Marxist-led campaign gained support, the union leaders were embarrassed into reluctantly getting involved. A larger campaign was developed to run a ballot initiative, Measure B, to slightly raise property taxes to save the county's Trauma Network which was on the verge of collapse and to save two hospitals slated for closing that were key components of this Trauma Network. Measure B won. Some 800,000 people use the public hospitals every year, predominately low income workers, immigrants and people of color. All the threatened jobs were saved, along with the Trauma Network and the two targeted hospitals. It was one of the first victories against neo-liberal austerity in the country.

Since the Marxists knew how capitalism functioned they knew there was enough money in Los Angeles County to make up the budget shortfall, and they had the commitment to do something about it. They then proposed a plan to meet their goals. Their initial plan was modified but a plan was developed and a campaigned waged. The Marxists were the ingredient that saved health services for hundreds of thousands of people, and saved thousands of health care workers' union jobs. Their Marxist analysis, combined with a union membership and community that wanted to stop the cutbacks and fight for social justice provided the synergy to win a big victory. Without the Marxists this would have been one more in a long line of defeats for workers, unions and the public, furthering demoralizing all of them. Instead, the victory gave great prestige to the union, and changed the relationship between the union and the employer, shifting a little more power to the union. The Marxists and socialists were not publicly known as Marxists, but rather as very good trade unionists with a good idea and a good plan. Many of them didn't want to make Marxism an issue among co-workers or the public since the remnants of a decades-long anti-socialism still influenced many people. Many more similar victories will lay a stronger foundation for more fundamental change, creating building blocks on the road to ultimately achieving a more humane society, socialism.

Turning Hardships into Victories

The biggest labor victories happened in the 1930's and 1940's when this same left strategy and practice was employed, only on a much larger scale. Here are a few of those stories.

One parallel today with labor's upsurge from that earlier period is that many of the workers struggling today to protect what they have (the Verizon workers and others), or fighting for much needed improvements (fast food workers), have a precarious job situation, just as many workers did in during the Great Depression. Precarious workers have instability in their jobs. They may be in established full-time jobs, like the Verizon workers other embattled workers, or in permanently precarious jobs as low wage workers, part-time workers, day laborers, temps, so-called "independent contractors," adjunct faculty, unemployed and underemployed, and students trying to find a job. It is this instability, fear, and struggle to survive that leads many precarious workers to become angry at the injustices in the system. They work hard, many went to school to improve their work skills and incurred high student debt, and now are told their job prospects are uncertain, their wages or benefits are going to be cut, and they may lose their jobs altogether. They have been battered by the normal functioning of capitalism and many are fighting mad. Many became the shock troops of the Occupy Wall Street movement, Black Lives Matter movement, and the Bernie Sanders campaign for president. Not only do they want immediate relief and answers to their daily problems, but they are increasingly searching for a more comprehensive explanation for why the system functions as it does.

When embattled workers, precarious workers, and victims of racism and other forms of discrimination begin to see that they have many common problems, and a common enemy, alliances and support for one another emerges. That is when their strength multiplies and bigger victories can be won. When these labor and social justice movements begin to understand that capitalism is responsible for much of their plight, and seek out the ideas and analysis of the Marxist left because it most effectively explains the injustices in the system, bigger victories will occur.

Big changes have taken place in the economy that have radically transformed the workforce. Most of the big factories that employed many thousands of workers in one location have long ago closed, so many workers today work in much smaller work groups. Many people believe that it is much harder, nearly impossible, to organize workers in such small work groups. But the Teamsters, and other unions, disproved this theory many, many decades ago. The Teamsters have many small work groups employed in thousands of locations across the country in cities, small towns and rural areas. Yet, the Teamsters are one of the largest unions in the country, with 1.4 million members. Deregulation of trucking and many other industries that began in the late 1970's dealt the Teamsters and other unions a hard blow. But all of these problems, including lack-luster top leaders in some unions, didn't stop Teamsters members and other unionists from fighting for justice on the job, organizing new members, and getting involved in social justice struggles. One big one was the 1980's victorious nationwide boycott of Coors beer (that I was involved in) because of the Coors corporation's anti-labor, racist, sexist, and right-wing practices. We won a big jobs creation program, especially for African Americans and Latinos. That is not to sugar-coat the problems, both internal and external. But these unions have persevered, in large part because progressives and leftists in these unions have fought to make our unions better fighters for the members, and fought for social justice causes as well, making us and our community allies stronger as we worked together.

Small work groups spread out in many different locations today should not be a deterrent in organizing workers into unions. What's needed is a good organizing plan. SEIU organized some 75,000 home health care workers into its union, people working in thousands of individual homes spread out across Los Angeles County, culminating in victory in 1999.

A look at history shows how much workers can accomplish when they face head-on serious grievances, have the will to fight, a progressive vision of justice, and good leadership that includes progressives, leftists and Marxists. While today's workers face issues and conditions that vary markedly from those facing workers in the 1930's and 1940's and beyond, there are a number of similarities: low pay, shrinking benefits, high costs for health care or no or inadequate healthcare, housing and other needs, an economic crash in 2008, job insecurity, racism and sexism, health and safety hazards, high pressure to produce at work, too few or too many hours of work, unstable work schedules, high unemployment and under employment, right-wing and anti-labor employers and other similar groups, and abusive bosses.

Social Justice Unionism and Youth

All of these issues and the Great Depression of the 1930's triggered massive protests and union organizing. The stock market crashed in 1929 and millions of people lost their jobs. This was a time when there were no social safety nets. (The corporations and anti-labor politicians today are eroding the social safety nets won then.) In 1930, the Communist Party initiated the formation of Unemployed Councils and in 1930 called for mass marches and rallies of the unemployed demanding immediate relief and jobs, breaking the demoralization and inaction of millions. The slogans for the marches were, "Don't Starve, Fight!" and "Work or Wages." A half a million (some say a million) unemployed marched in New York, Pittsburgh, Buffalo, Cleveland, Milwaukee, Detroit, Chicago, Denver, Los Angeles, San Francisco, Seattle and other cities. These mass demonstrations, by people who would be called the precariat today, became the shock troops of a broader movement that led to the organization of unions in the mid and late 1930's, and laws that created unemployment insurance, jobs creation programs like the Works Progress Administration (WPA), and other social programs. During the Great Depression no one would have predicted that the destitute down-and-out unemployed would be the participants and even among the leaders of the mass movement for jobs, unemployment insurance and relief, food programs and other social programs, and unionization. But the political left did.

The union organizing upsurge of the 1930's was also led by Communists, Socialists and others under the umbrella of the Congress of Industrial Organization (CIO). The CIO brought 6 million workers into industrial unions, and millions more joined the generally more conservative AFL- affiliated unions. Many of the left-led unions then elected their leftist leaders to union office, including socialists and communists. Under this leftwing and Marxist leadership, many of the new unions not only organized and negotiated big improvements in wages, benefits, and working conditions for their members, but they fought for larger social justice issues, such as against racism in the labor movement and in the larger society. Over a half million African American workers joined CIO unions, breaking the color bar in the trade union movement. Then, Black union leaders, like socialist A. Philip Randolph of the Sleeping Car Porters union and other Black union members, laid the foundation for the civil rights movement of the 1950's. (See the new book, The Struggle for a Substantive Democracy, published by the Committees of Correspondence Education Fund for more information on how the labor movement and African-Americans united to advance democracy and achieve big improvements in the lives of both of groups and the general public then and at other key junctures in the life of our country.)

Longshore workers prior to 1934 were precarious workers, forced to stand in the humiliating early morning "shape-up" where bosses handpicked the workers they wanted to work that day. The others were sent home. Some of the most desperate and downtrodden begged to be picked for work, and many had to give kickbacks from their pay to the bosses who picked them. They were low paid, precariously employed, and many lived in deep poverty. Some people derogatorily called longshoremen of that era "rats of the wharf," scrambling across the wharf trying to get work. In 1934, the leaders of a union organizing drive, led by Harry Bridges, a leftist and Marxist working with the Communist Party, launched a longshore workers strike that shut down the entire west coast. In San Francisco, workers in other industries joined in a General Strike. A huge strike committee ran the city for three days, giving tens of thousands a taste of workers power, an element of socialism.

The strike was won, and the longshore workers union, the International Longshore and Warehouse Union (ILWU), was recognized by the employers. The union was so strong that it won a union-operated hiring hall. Gone was the demeaning and discriminatory company "shape-up", and ILWU longshore workers were now dispatched to load and unload ships in a fair rotation from the hiring hall. Communists and other leftists were important organizers in forming the union, and negotiating such pro-worker language in the contract with the shippers. After winning big improvements in wages, benefits, working conditions, workers' rights, the longshore workers were now called the "Lords of the Docks." ILWU jobs are held in high esteem in port cities all along the pacific coast today.

The ILWU also engages in social justice activity. During the war in Vietnam in the 1960's and 1970's, and the war in Iraq in the 2000's, ILWU members shut down west coast ports in one day strikes to demand an end to these wars.   The ILWU still has battles with shippers because of the inherent nature of capitalism that drives companies to cut costs and maximize profits on the backs of workers and the community. But with the ILWU and its progressive ideology and fighting history longshore workers have a fighting chance to protect their hard won gains. The struggles of the ILWU are one of the reasons the San Francisco Bay area is a region of progressivism that continues to this day.

After the financial capitalist elite crashed the economy in 2008, a predominately young leftist-oriented precariat occupied Wall Street in New York City and then many other cities and demanded that the 1% on Wall Street stop fleecing the 99% everywhere else. Unbridled police brutality and murder of predominately African American young men sparked big protests and the formation of the Black Lives Matter Movement. And a generation of young people, sick of being frozen out of a good lives and facing growing unmet needs came together with many others to spark the mass outpouring of support for the presidential campaign of Bernie Sanders.   Many of these young people from these and other social justice movements became the organizers and shock troops of Bernie's political revolution. In every state where Bernie ran he won the majority of the votes of people 45 years and younger. Polls showed that 80% of millennials who voted, voted for Bernie Sanders. Millennials, born between 1982 and 2000, number 83 million people. These young people are the future of our country.

Activists in all these movements are smart, politically progressive to leftwing or socialist, bold, creative, and involved, and in their majority working-class. As they continue to connect the dots, deepen their political understanding of how capitalism exploits and abuses, reach out to more of their peers, develop plans to fight racism and all forms of discrimination, work to invigorate the labor movement, and learn more organizational tools and strategies, they will become an even greater force for progressive social change. We should continue our work with these committed activists to help build the kind of movement that can change society.

Paul Krehbiel is a former union auto worker, Teamster, union organizer, local union president, and chief negotiator for 5,000 Registered Nurses (members of SEIU in Los Angeles County). He was active in US Labor against the War, a coordinator of Los Angeles Labor for Bernie, and is Co-Chair of the Labor Committee of CCDS.

Workers Memorial Day

By Frank Rosenthal

Workers Memorial Day honors workers who
have died due to unsafe workplaces.1   It
was observed on April 28, this year, a few
weeks after a historic first: the CEO of a
major US corporation was sentenced to
prison for conspiring to violate safety rules
resulting in worker deaths.   The CEO is
Don Blankenship of Massey Coal Company
where 29 workers died in a mine explosion
in 2010. It was the worst US mining disaster in 40 years.

We know that the attitude and behavior of
the top executive of a company greatly affects safety in the workplace.
So the Blankenship conviction is welcome and important. Such convictions almost never happen because of weak laws and the fact that layers of subordinates can obscure the connection between the CEO and
workplace conditions.   But Blankenship was different. He obsessively
micromanaged the company and left a conspicuous trail of memos telling mangers to forget about upgrading safety systems and instead "run
coal". In other words he told the people in charge to put profits ahead
of saving lives.

In light of this extreme and blatant situation the US Department of Justice stepped in.   Blankenship was indicted not under the weak OSHA
criminal statues, but under federal anti-conspiracy law.

The same factor of putting profits ahead of safety is behind deaths and injuries taking place every day -- the back injuries among health care workers because they are lifting patients without adequate staff and equipment, because profit margins don't allow it, the farmworkers who die
because they are paid on piece rate, and have to cut corners and work fast
to make a living wage. The construction workers who die in falls because
management does not require that they wear proper fall protection.

Last year, worker safety was sacrificed to profits with two ominous trends...

First, the number of workers paid on temporary arrangements through contracts and agencies continued to increase. These workers often get no training or safety equipment. Because of blurred lines of management responsibility, OSHA regulations are often not enforced, and there are high rates of fatalities and injuries.

Second, under the guise of reform, state workers compensation systems are being gutted. Benefits have decreased, reducing the insurance premiums that companies pay. And a new corporate alliance led an effort to get states to privatize workers compensation giving employers the power to circumvent state regulations entirely.

Today, as before, the only thing that stands in the way of these dangerous trends is the workers movements, their organizations and their progressive allies. One hundred five years ago, Rose Schneiderman, a young labor organizer made this point to a mass meeting of workers, and their middle and upper class supporters a few days after the Triangle Shirtwaist Factory Fire, in which 146 young workers died due to abysmal safety conditions. The meeting became tense as workers tired of hearing platitudes from politicians, professors and religious leaders.

Then Schneiderman spoke:

"I would be a traitor to these poor burned bodies if I came here to talk good fellowship. We have tried you good people of the public and we have found you wanting.. This is not the first time girls have been burned alive in the city. Every week I must learn of the untimely death of one of my sister workers. Every year thousands of us are maimed. The life of men and women is so cheap and property is so sacred. There are so many of us for one job it matters little if 146 of us are burned to death. "...Public officials have only words of warning to us—warning that we must be intensely peaceable, and they have the workhouse just back of all their warnings. The strong hand of the law beats us back, when we rise, into the conditions that make life unbearable.

"I can't talk fellowship to you who are gathered here. Too much blood has been spilled. I know from my experience it is up to the working people to save themselves. The only way they can save themselves is by a strong working-class movement."

Three days later, hundreds of thousands filled the streets of New York in mourning and protest. In the next two years, thirty-six new safety laws and regulations were enacted.

Let the memory of those who lost their lives at work last year inspire us to fulfill the promise made by OSHA, 45 years ago, "to assure ... every working man and woman in the Nation safe and healthful working conditions".

1. A good source of information about worker deaths and injuries is the yearly report by the AFL-CIO (http://www.aflcio.org/Issues/Job-Safety/ Death-on-the-Job-Report). In 2014 (the last year for which complete data is available) 4821 workers were killed due to traumatic injuries. The rate per 100,000 increased from the previous year (3.4 vs. 3.3). It is estimated that 50,000 people died from occupational diseases. There were nearly 3.8 million occupational injuries reported. See the above link for other relevant info.

Frank Rosenthal is a professor at Purdue University.

Unions Win Safer Jobs for Working People

By Rebecca L. Reindel and M.K. Fletcher
Reprinted from the AFL-CIO

For centuries, unions have been at the forefront of fighting for and winning safer protections for working people. Horrific workplace tragedies such as the Triangle Shirtwaist Factory and the Hawks Nest Tunnel disasters are reminders of the need for unions.

Unions fought for the passage of the Occupational Safety and Health Act of 1970, which created the Occupational Safety and Health Administration. Over the past 45 years, unions have won national and state safety and health protections for all working people, including key standards such as asbestos, benzene, lead, confined spaces and fall protection; and now more than 532,000 working people can say their lives have been saved through this law.

These protections benefit every worker on the job, not just union members. Bottom of Form Unions also win strong collective bargaining contracts in their workplaces, establishing key safety protections such as safety representatives and labor management committees, as well as other labor protections such as higher wages, retirement security, work autonomy, job security, paid time off and predictable scheduling.

Unions are still winning important protections for all people by advocating for and defending safety and health standards.

In March, OSHA issued the most important health rule in 30 years. These comprehensive silica standards will save more than 600 lives and prevent more than 900 cases of silicosis (and other chronic diseases) each year, by using common sense controls like water and vacuums to reduce exposure in construction, maritime and general industries.

Just a few weeks ago, OSHA updated its injury and illness recordkeeping requirements, requiring companies to electronically submit their

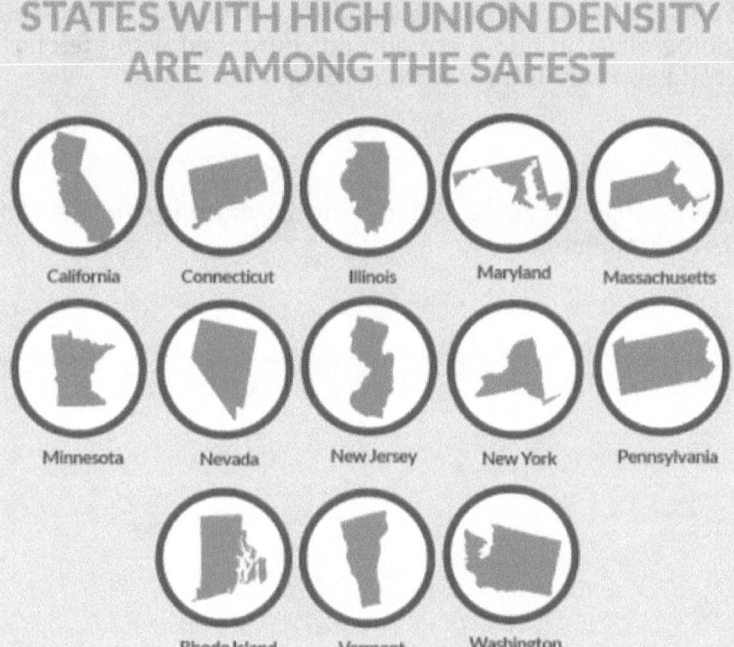

STATES WITH HIGH UNION DENSITY ARE AMONG THE SAFEST

California   Connecticut   Illinois   Maryland   Massachusetts

Minnesota   Nevada   New Jersey   New York   Pennsylvania

Rhode Island   Vermont   Washington

Thirteen states rank in the top 20 in both union density and lowest rates of workplace fatalities.

Sources: U.S. Bureau of Labor Statistics, 2014; AFL-CIO Death on the Job—The Toll of Neglect, 2016

AFL-CIO

injury and illness logs to an online OSHA database regularly. Because of this record-keeping update, working people and employers can better identify workplace hazards causing injury and illness in their industries and at their worksites. Importantly, this rule increases anti-retaliation protections to help workers report injuries and illnesses without fear of employer repercussions.

While these protections are success stories for working people, we still have work to do. The new OSHA rules, as well as other new labor protections, are under attack from wealthy big business lobbyists and right-wing politicians.

Additionally, more states have "right to work" laws, which weaken safety and health working conditions, than ever before. Workers in states with right to work laws are at a 49% greater risk of dying on the job, and states with greater union density also tend to have lower job fatality rates.

Unions are critical in the push for stronger safety and health protections and to keep the protections workers have—making sure that profits are not put ahead of working people's right to provide for their families and return home alive, in one piece and not burdened with lifelong illness. Unions will keep winning for working people.

Reference

http://www.aflcio.org/Blog/Organizing-Bargaining/Unions-Win-Safer-Jobs-for-Working-People

Youth: Searching for a Future

A Revolutionary Perspective: Anarchist Socialism...through Marxism

By Alex Krehbiel

This is written primarily for my fellow millennial brothers and sisters who are in the revolutionary socialist movements and who are attracted to anarchism and anarchist ways of working. First, there is much value in the anarchist tradition. Anarchists advocate and practice political bold-ness, direct action, organizing and empowerment from the grassroots, and see anarchism as a direct and pure way to create a new society that is free from exploitation, bureaucracy and the corruption that too often results from those in power.   These are all very positive and have broad support across the entire left, including among Marxist socialists, which is my ideological base. The key question is how do we make this new society happen?

Many anarchists believe that the only way we can achieve an egalitarian anarchist socialism is by an immediate end to all authoritative govern-ment because it is inherently in conflict with equality and an egalitarian society. This leads many to reject participation in elections, for example, because they are a part of this hierarchical, unequal, and unjust system. If you can convince everyone to embrace your vision of anarchist social-ism, we are part of the way there. If you can't, how will you succeed? You need a strategy.

Marxists believe this proposition is impractical for a number of reasons. One problem is how will you build and lead a revolutionary movement without organization, structure and leadership? Once a revolution is successful how do you carry out all the intricate functions of society de-void of some organizational structure, including follow-up and account-ability to make sure that tasks are done, and done correctly?   It also seems unlikely that people's thoughts, beliefs and attitudes will suddenly shift from capitalistically trained individualism and selfishness to socialistically inclined selflessness without a period of time to allow socialist education, practices and laws to win over the vast majority of the people living in a society or country that is trying to create a socialist society.

Spanish Syndicalist Poster 1933: Our Watchword is Freedom!

Given these problems, Marxists believe that it's not possible to build a successful revolutionary movement, make a successful revolution, and create a socialist society with anarchistic spontaneity alone. History does not reveal any anarchist-led revolutions that have been able to usher in a sustained socialism. A number of Marxists and socialists have different ideas on how to get to socialism. Some socialists believe such a society can only be reached through the immediate dissolution of all government, hierarchy or authority. For many of these anarchist socialists, it does not matter if this happens through violence or peaceful means, just so long as it happens. (Some stains of anarchism don't espouse socialism.)

There are also different varieties of socialists. Some are Marxists. Marxists led the revolutions in Russia, China, Vietnam, Cuba and other countries which had communists-led governments. The main difference between Anarchist socialists and Marxist socialists is over our different approaches to getting to revolutionary socialism. Our end goals are the same. We each favor different strategies and tactics to wage the revolutionary struggle, and we have different conceptions of what the transition from revolution to socialism will look like and how socialism will function.

A significant number of Marxist-led socialist revolutions did succeed in ushering in a form of sustained socialism. Their weaknesses, and constant attacks from global capitalism, led many, but not all to collapse. Yet, even with their problems and eventual collapse, these socialist societies did achieve important gains for millions of people. We have something to learn from this history, including the development and role that Communist parties played in these socialist revolutions and in developing socialist societies. We must study the mistakes and in some cases terrible abuses, as well as the positive developments. And we must realize that we are all in this together. The capitalists class that we are up against has much power, through their control of businesses, the schools, the news media, most of the TV industry and much of the film industry, the police and courts, many government bodies, and others. We have to find ways to work together, to build a united movement. You can get to anarchism, but I'd like to suggest that adopting some Marxist practices can help the process immensely.

Socialist Unity

Boston Socialist Unity Project Conference Aims at Left Cooperation

By Donald Donato

May 2 2016 - BOSTON - Local poet John Greenleaf Whittier once wrote, "So long as Boston shall Boston be, and her bay tides rise and fall, shall freedom stand in the Old South Church, and plead for the rights of all." Fittingly, this historic venue opened its doors on Saturday, April 30th, for the first conference of the Boston Socialist Unity Project (BSUP1). It was an extraordinary gathering of local and regional activists for a day full of learning and sharing, of theory and practice - all focused on building the movement for a society based on dignity and human rights for all.

Seeking to bring about unity through collective projects and educational events, BSUP1 was held under the theme: "Building Socialism. Building Our Movements." It brought together socialists and activists from a variety of organizations in the Boston area to discuss common areas of work and ways to strengthen each other's efforts in the long-term goal of replacing capitalism with a more just economic and social system.

Unity in the making

The idea of BSUP was first raised in November 2014 with a talk among local socialist activists about what a minimum level of practical unity between them might look like. While the question of electoral work can often be a divisive one among people who come from different left-wing traditions, social and educational initiatives tend to be areas where more agreement can be reached.

With this in mind, leaders of the local affiliates of the Communist Party USA (CPUSA), Committees of Correspondence for Democracy and Socialism (CCDS), and Solidarity were chosen to form a "continuations committee", to further explore areas of possible cooperation. This committee organized the September 2015 event, "Jacobin, Young Radicals, and Left Unity," with Bhaskar Sunkara and Karen Narefsky, at the SEIU 615 Local in Boston. The question which emerged from this meeting was how to build socialism while also building activist movements.

This weekend's BSUP1 conference was convened to take on this challenge, and it involved a wide range of organizations: Boston for Bernie; Boston Solidarity; Center for Marxist Education; Color of Water Project; Committee for International Labor Defense; CCDS; Communist Party of Greater Boston (CPUSA); Democratic Socialists of America; Freedom Road Socialist Organization; Global Zero; International Socialist Organization; Jill Stein for President; July 26th Coalition for Solidarity with Cuba; Mass Global Action; Mass Campaign to Abolish Poverty; Socialism and Democracy; Socialist Alternative; Socialist Party USA; System Change Not Climate Change; United for Justice with Peace; Venezuela Solidarity Committee; and Workers World Party.

Socialism no longer a taboo

The Communist Party of Greater Boston's Casey Doyle opened the morning plenary by reflecting on current events:

"We find ourselves in an exciting time. In 2016, socialism is no longer the taboo word it once was. More and more people are joining social movements and demanding a better world. This renewed discussion has led us to the question of what socialism looks like today: what it is, what it isn't, what it could be."

Speaking of the struggle to find unity among the disparate socialist traditions, Doyle said, "While we must look to history to guide us, we often get caught up in arguments of the past and lose sight of our common goal: a future society based on human need and not based on the unending drive for profit."

Noting how easy it is to get lost and burned out running from one action or meeting to another, opening panelist Cynthia Peters (LeftRoots) poignantly posed the fundamental question: "How do we connect our day-to-day struggles for people in the community with a larger social and political strategy?" She suggested that one of the central means of overcoming this challenge is to plug organizing into a larger social and political agenda.

According to another speaker, Jorge Márin of the Venezuela Solidarity Committee, one of the key tasks of building a movement capable of taking socialists to another level of influence and power is to reach out and organize with diverse communities - particularly African Americans, Latinos, and others - locally, nationally, and internationally.

Building on this idea, the Marxist historian and author, Dr. Vijay Prashad from Trinity College in Hartford implored the conference to recognize and remedy the "deep fragmentation of the American left, in political, theoretical, and organizational terms."

While brandishing a copy of Marx's Capital, Dr. Prashad appealed for a return to "theory rooted in movement," and said that in building working class power, "actions...are a means to an end, which is working class power." Emphasizing that "No worker is an abstraction," Prashad said, "they all have multiple identities, so that racism is not just an issue for African Americans, it is a threat to working class power; misogyny is not just a threat to women, but to the essential feminism of working class power; as the Knights of Labor's motto unequivocally demanded: 'An injury to one is an injury to all!'"

Putting words into action

To begin building just such a working class movement, the conference conducted workshops to discuss theory, action, and strategy. The "ABCs of Socialism," facilitated by Jacobin editor Nicole Aschoff, looked at the success of Jacobin magazine and the new wave of Millennials who are thirsty for an introduction to the socialist movement and are looking for ways to participate in it.

"Feminism and Socialism," led by Monica Poole of Bunker Hill Community College, took an intersectional and interactive approach to engaging with feminism. Any preparation for a working class movement must also be practically prepared for state persecution and police brutality, which the "Origins of Police" workshop, convened by Nino Brown of Mass Action, discussed both in terms of political activism and racism. "Secrets of a Successful Organizer," presented by Chris Brooks and Dan DiMaggio from Labor Notes, featured an interactive look at successfully moving people into action.

Vijay Prashad gave the workshop "U.S. Imperialism: Past and Present," a look back at classical imperialism and its relationship to monopoly stage capitalism. He compared it with current trends of commodity chains and intellectual property rights which have transformed the basis of imperialism in the 21st century. Finally, Chris Williams of System Change Not Climate Change engaged participants on actions to stop the horrific

damage capitalism is inflicting on the environment in the workshop, "What is Eco-Socialism?"

An integral theme of the conference, which seemed to emerge organically, was the collective realization of the need to begin building parallel organizations of working class power in the Boston area. Along this strategic line of development, the very existence of the conference - the fruit of over two years of cooperation between local groups - is but one example.

Conference organizers are looking to continue the momentum of BSUP1 by beginning work to set up a Boston Socialist School and coordinating actions to support local labor and solidarity campaigns, like the Verizon workers. A meeting to follow up on the work and findings of the conference will take place on May 14, where planning will also begin for BSUP2 slated for 2017.

For more detailed information, visit the Boston Socialist Unity Project website.

Donald Donato is a writer, priest, and human services advocate from Boston. He has worked with community-based organizations in support of economic, social, and cultural rights as human rights for over 20 years, and he is currently the Area Planner and grant writer for an Area Agency on Aging near Boston.

Photo: Donald Donato/PW

Organizing the Boston Socialist Unity Conference 2016: A New Path?

By Duncan McFarland

The social and environmental problems of the times are serious and urgent, and the Left needs to be much stronger. Surely, fragmentation of Left forces is a major reason for its lack of power, yet calls for left unity have yielded limited results. Do the Next Left and 21st century socialism have an answer?

I have been part of a number of left or progressive unity events in recent years. Some programs were very good, yet every effort fizzled out. Sometimes the goals for unity seemed too ambitious for the immediate prospects; the challenge is to create a process that sustains and builds.

CCDS-Boston initiated an activist discussion on strengthening the movement with Bill Fletcher, who was visiting town in Nov. 2014. The meeting was invitation only to facilitate discussion. Several socialist organizations and a number of individuals participated in the standing-room only event. The conversation moved to consideration of the minimum principles of unity for joint work.

CCDS-Boston organized a follow-up meeting with Carl Davidson on the theme of basic principles of unity. This meeting formed a continuations committee with representatives from CCDS, the Communist Party and Solidarity. A public program was proposed featuring speakers from Jacobin magazine, as something fresh, already successful in attracting a substantial sector of the movement, and to bring youth to balance the "68er" skewing of the earlier meetings.

A name was needed for the sponsor. Should the focus be socialist, anti-imperialist, radical, Left, or whatever? Finally "Boston Socialist Unity Project" was agreed on; consciously socialist, while inviting others to participate, and a concrete project orientation rather than forming a new organization. We called ourselves a generic "group" rather than a coalition. Our first public program, featuring Jacobin editor and publisher Bhaskar Sunkara, was well-attended and successful.

The next step was setting the goal of organizing a one-day socialist conference in the Spring of 2016. In Boston, there have been socialist conferences in past years but always sponsored by one specific organization. A conference co-sponsored by a number of different socialist organizations -- and including individuals -- would be unprecedented and represent an advance towards unity.

Turnout at the organizing meetings was good including many youth and people with different socialist politics. What did we stand for? How could the group maintain unity? A description of BSUP was written with generic socialist language. All self-identified socialists were invited to participate equally. The informal rule was that no one could attack someone else's concept of socialism while of course free to explain their own viewpoint. The meetings evolved a friendly spirit with little bickering or friction. Soon millennials became a majority of the organizing group and brought their style, horizontal and inclusive. They refused to be divided over electoral politics; participants included people in the Sanders Democratic primary campaign and those advocating independent politics.

What was the goal of the conference? It was very important to the millennials in particular that the whole range of socialist groups in Boston should all participate. More and more groups joined in the work until the entire range of socialist groups in Boston were participating, including those focused on working with mainstream progressives to leftwing cadre organizations.

While notions of "thinking the unthinkable," mergers and breakthroughs had at times been advanced, these struck me as long term goals not practical in the short run. I proposed, "elevate the level of cooperation" as an organizing guideline. Actual left unity was too ambitious -- people can object with many reasons for not creating unity -- but it was hard to disagree with more -- lots more -- cooperation.

Consequently, an important goal of the conference from my perspective was forming a group of organizers, and relationship-building; are there organizations and people willing and capable of working together productively to sustain motion towards more cooperation and collaboration? A one-off success did not interest me -- how to keep things going?

The conference would focus on socialist political education while also featuring workshops on local struggles that people could join. Learning from the social forum methods, there would be no effort to reach consensus on an action program or campaign that would engender divisive debate. An educational format could accommodate different political views in various presentations or workshops. The question of joint work in mass struggles would be considered at a later point. Ideas that all could support were proposed: working on the May Day rally, supporting striking workers, running a candidate in a nonpartisan election.

An immediate goal was founding a Boston socialist school; this could be a vehicle for continuing the organizing in the interim before the second conference in 2017. Unity could be maintained as diverse socialist perspectives could organize their own classes. The school would support existing Left educational programs and so would begin with an extensive consultation process, creating a calendar and listing resources. Organizers of the New York Marxist education project and the former Brecht Forum drove up to attend the conference, sharing valuable experiences.

The conference itself completely filled two floors of Old South Church. Left Roots led the morning plenary with a speech on its principles and announcing its Boston branch. Popular workshops included a debate on elections with Labor for Bernie and the Green Party, and the ABCs of socialism presented by Jacobin magazine. The Verizon workers called out for support. The breadth of political participation was unprecedented in anyone's memory. Considerable challenges lay ahead for the second conference: better outreach and a theme for the program.

Reflecting on the goals, the conference was a unique accomplishment, with an abundance of comradely spirit and practical cooperation. However, it can only be considered a good first step. Were we successful in opening up a new approach to advance the effort towards left unity, a style bearing the stamp of the Next Left? Will the most important need, a group continuing to work together collectively and productively, actually materialize? Will the Boston socialist school remain a vision or become a reality? The next year should tell whether we can sustain this new left unity initiative.

Section 4. 2016 Elections

EDITOR'S NOTE:This issue of Dialogue & Initiative closes with a retro-
spective and introductory look at the many "firsts" of the 2016 general
election cycle.

Seize the Moment: Bernie Sanders and Building the Progressive Majority

By Harry Targ

The multiracial working class in alliance with trade unions, women, African Americans, Latinos and other people of color, youth, and progressive sectors of business now form the promising components of the progressive majority. The profound challenge before the working class and its allies is to organize this majority into a coherent force capable of responding to the various issues it confronts. ("Goals and Principles," Committees of Correspondence for Democracy and Socialism, adopted at its 6th National Convention, July, 2009, www.cc-ds.org).

Protest Movements in the United States

In addition to anecdotal evidence, aggregate data confirms the continuation and expansion of activist groups and protest activities all across the face of the globe. For example in the United States, Mark Solomon in an important essay "Whither the Socialist Left? Thinking the 'Unthinkable'" (March 6, 2013, www.portside.org) discusses the long history of socialism in the United States, the brutal repression against it, damaging sectarian battles on the left, the miniscule size of socialist organizations today and yet paradoxically the growing sympathy for the idea of socialism among Americans, particularly young people. He calls for "the convergence of socialist organizations committed to non-sectarian democratic struggle, engagement with mass movements, and open debate in search of effective responses to present crises and to projecting a socialist future." The Solomon article does not conceptualize "left unity" and "building the progressive majority" as separate and distinct projects but as fundamentally interconnected. For him, and many others, the role of the left in the labor movement and other mass movements gave shape, direction, and theoretical cohesion to the battles that won worker rights in the 1930s.

Solomon's call has stimulated debate among activists around the idea of "left unity." The appeal for left unity is made more powerful by socialism's appeal, the current global crises of capitalism, rising mobilizations around the world, and living experiments with small-scale socialism such as the construction of a variety of workers' cooperatives.

Effective campaigns around "left unity" in recent years have prioritized "revolutionary education," drawing upon the tools of the internet to construct an accessible body of theory and debate about strategy and tactics that could solidify left forces and move the progressive majority into a socialist direction. The emerging Online University of the Left (OUL), an electronic source for classical and modern theoretical literature about Marxism, contemporary debates about strategy and tactics, videos, reading lists, and course syllabi, constitute one example of left unity. The OUL serves as one of many resources for study groups, formal coursework, and discussions among socialists and progressives. Those who advocate for "left unity" or left "convergence" celebrate these many developments, from workers cooperatives to popular education, as they advocate for the construction of a unified socialist left.

A second manifestation of political activism, the Occupy Movement, first surfacing in the media in September, 2011, initiated and renewed traditions of organized and spontaneous mass movements around issues that affect peoples' immediate lives such as housing foreclosure, debt, jobs, wages, the environment, and the negative role of money in U.S. politics. Perhaps the four most significant contributions of the Occupy Movement have been:

1.Introducing grassroots processes of decision-making.

2.Conceptualizing modern battles for social and economic justice as between the one percent (the holders of most wealth and power in society) versus the 99 percent (weak, economically marginalized, and dispossessed, including the "precariat").

3.Insisting that struggles for radical change be spontaneous, often eschewing traditional political processes.

4.Linking struggles locally, nationally, and globally.

During the height of its visibility some 500 cities and towns experienced Occupy mobilizations around social justice issues. While less frequent, Occupy campaigns still exist, particularly in cities where larger progressive communities reside. Calls for left unity correctly ground their claims in a long and rich history of organized struggle while "occupiers" and other activists today have been inspired by the bottom-up and spontaneous uprisings of 2011 (both international and within the United States).

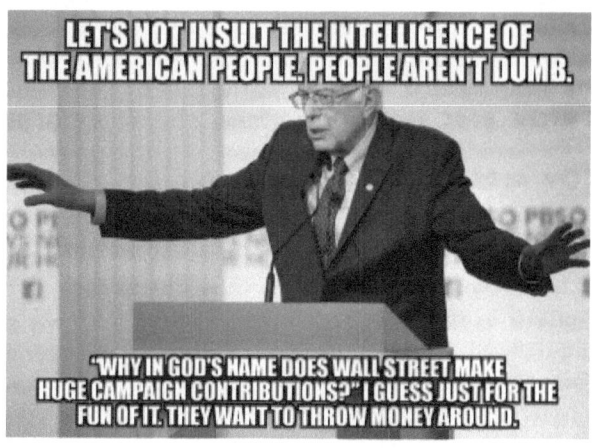

A third, and not opposed, approach to political change at this time has been labeled "building a progressive majority." This approach assumes that large segments of the U.S. population agree on a variety of issues. Some are activists in electoral politics, others in trade unions, and more in single issue groups. In addition, many who share common views of worker rights, the environment, health care, undue influence of money in politics, immigrant rights etc. are not active politically. The progressive majority perspective argues that the project for the short-term is to mobilize the millions of people who share common views on the need for significant if not fundamental change in economics and politics.

Often organizers conceptualize the progressive majority as the broad mass of people who share views on politics and economics that are 'centrist" or "left." Consequently, over the long run, "left" participants see their task as three-fold. First, they must work on the issues that concern majorities of those at the local and national level. Second, they struggle to convince their political associates that the problems most people face have common causes (particularly capitalism). Third, "left" participants see the need to link issues so that class, race, gender, and the environment, for example, are understood as part of the common problem that people face.

A 2005-2007 data set called "Start" (startguide.org) showed that there were some "500 leading organizations in the United States working for progressive change on a national level." START divided these 500 organizations into twelve categories based on their main activities. These included progressive electoral, peace and foreign policy, economic justice, civil liberties, health advocacy, labor, women's and environmental organizations. Of course, their membership, geographic presence, financial resources, and strategic and tactical vision varied widely. And, many of the variety of progressive organizations at the national level were reproduced at the local and state levels as well.

In sum, when looking at contemporary social change in the United States at least three tendencies have been articulated: left unity, the Occupy Movement, and building a progressive majority. Each highlights its own priorities as to vision, strategy, tactics, and political contexts. In addition, the relative appeal of each may be affected by age, class, gender, race, and issue prioritization as well. However, these approaches need not be seen as contradictory. Rather the activism borne of each approach may parallel the others. (the discussion of the three tendencies of activism appeared in Harry Targ, "The Fusion Politics Response to 21st Century Imperialism From Arab Spring to Moral Mondays," ouleft.org, and was presented at the "Moving Beyond Capitalism" Conference, Center for Global Justice, San Miguel de Allende Mexico, July 29-August 5, 2014).

Building the Progressive Majority in 2016

The statement above from CCDS was published in 2009 and the description of the three political tendencies in the United States was presented in 2014. Since then, the Moral Mondays Movement in North Carolina captured national attention and stimulated a growing campaign around Reverend William Barber's narrative of United States history referring to the "three reconstructions" and the articulation of his theory of "fusion politics."

The egregious police violence against African Americans, particularly young men and women of color, has sparked a vibrant Black Lives Matter campaign that has caused a renewed interest in understanding the functions the police serve, the role of white supremacy, rightwing populism, and Michelle Alexander's "New Jim Crow" in America.

Militant workers in growing sectors of the economy are rising up. Fast food workers are organizing around the "Fight for 15." Health and home care, and other service sector workers are demanding the right to have their unions recognized. And teachers, transportation workers, and state employees have hit the streets and legislative assemblies to demand worker rights.

The peace movement has begun to resuscitate itself challenging a new cold war with Russia, boots on the ground and drones in the air to fight ISIS, and the unbridled growth of the military/industrial complex.

Finally, environmentalists have made a convincing case that the connection between neoliberal global capitalism and environmental catastrophe "changes everything."

The three tendencies presented above-left unity, the Occupy Movement, and building a progressive majority-continue to be reflected in different kinds of organizing around the country based on the issues, levels of organization, predominant ideological manifestations, local political cultures, and the composition of movements in different places based upon class, race, gender, sexual identity, religious affiliation and issue orientation. And all these tendencies are worthy of attention and support, particularly in the 21st century "time of chaos."

But a new campaign (potentially a movement) emerged during the summer, 2015. Bernie Sanders, an aging left-oriented Senator from Vermont began his long uphill march to secure the Democratic Party nomination for the presidency. A sixties activist on civil rights and peace, a populist mayor of Burlington, Vermont, a Congressman and Senator from that state, Sanders, since his early days of political activism, has articulated an anti-Wall Street, anti-finance capital mantra that has its roots in various progressive currents in United States history, These include the populist campaigns of the 1890s, the militant workers struggles of the Wobblies during the Progressive era, the popular electoral campaigns of five-time Socialist Party candidate for President, Eugene V. Debs from 1900 to 1920; the industrial union movement of the 1930s which built the Congress of Industrial Organizations (CIO) and support for the New Deal legislation that provided some measure of economic security to many workers; to the civil rights and anti-war movements of the 1960s and beyond.

Sanders has proceeded to excoriate finance capital and to link the enormous accumulation of wealth and income at one pole of American society and the maintenance and growth of the misery of the masses on the other. He has advanced his narrative by linking class, to race, to gender issues, and has begun to incorporate the apocalyptic possibilities of a future without addressing climate change. In a word, he has articulated a program that the CCDS program defined as the vision of "the progressive majority."

The vision of a progressive majority is one that emphasizes the systematic articulation of the causes of human misery and what needs to be done to overcome them and the belief that the vision already exists among the majority of the American people. So far, the popularity of the Sanders campaign, the particular enthusiasm it is generating at the grassroots, including from youth, labor, feminist, anti-racist, and environmental organizations, and the demographics reflected in his primary victories in over twenty states, suggest that activists from the three tendencies identified above should direct their energies to supporting the Sanders presidential run.

Most importantly, the Sanders campaign has inspired the possibility of building a long-standing progressive movement that will survive and grow beyond the Democratic Convention in July and the November,

2016 election. Even Candidate Sanders suggests that his campaign is emblematic of a "political revolution." While clear media and party machinations have made a Sanders victory all but impossible, debate has begun among progressives about how to use the energy and organization of the Sanders campaign to build a broader movement. In sum, the Sanders campaign may be the most significant organized manifestation for building left unity dialogue and building a progressive majority.

www.heartlandradical.blogspot.com

For the People, Not the Billionaires Bernie Sanders for President 2016

Published by LA Labor for Bernie

1. Rebuild crumbling infrastructure. Invest $1 trillion to repair roads, bridges, water systems, schools, and other public facilities, which would create 13 million good paying jobs.

2. Racial justice. Demilitarize the police, prosecute police crimes, and establish community control of the police. Stop disenfranchisement of people of color voters, and fund a $5.5 billion federal jobs program for youth, with a focus on those suffering most – Black and brown youth.

3. Reverse climate change. The US should be a world leader in transitioning away from polluting fossil fuels and into energy efficient wind, solar, geothermal, and biomass to create millions of green jobs.

4. Create worker co-ops. Create businesses that workers own and operate, increasing quality and worker contentment, instead of giving huge tax breaks to corporations who ship jobs overseas.

5. Grow the union movement. Union workers bargain for and have won higher wages and benefits than non-union workers. Pass a law that will give workers a union when a majority sign union authorization cards.

6. Raise the current minimum wage. Double the national minimum wage to $15 an hour. No one who works 40 hours a week should live in poverty.

7. Pay equity for women. Women earn 78 percent of men for compa-rable work. We need equal pay for equal work.

8. Fair trade. Since 2001 we have lost more than 60,000 factories and nearly 5 million manufacturing jobs to overseas low wage countries. End disastrous trade policies (NAFTA, CAFTA and others) and stop the Trans Pacific Partnership to save jobs.

9. Make college affordable for all. Free tuition at public colleges and re-duce massive student debt so students are trained for good jobs without facing financial burdens.

10. Take on Wall Street. Six huge financial institutions have assets equal to 61% of our gross domestic product – over $9.8 trillion. They plunged our country into the Great Recession of 2008. Too-big-to-fail banks need to be broken up.

11. Healthcare for All. Forty million Americans have no health insurance, yet we spend twice as much per capita as any other country. We need an improved Medicare for All single-payer system.

12. Protect the most vulnerable. Millions of seniors and children live in poverty. We must strengthen Social Security, Medicare, Medicaid and nutrition programs.

13. Real Tax reform. With massive income and wealth inequality, we need a progressive tax system based on ability to pay. Some major cor-porations pay nothing in federal income taxes, and many stash cash in offshore tax havens, costing our country $100 billion a year. This must be stopped, and everyone must pay their fair share.

14. Restore democracy/overturn Citizens United. Stop billionaires from buying elections.

Why Progressives Need an Electoral Strategy-and Fast

By Bill Fletcher, Jr.
AlterNet

April 12, 2016.   Every electoral cycle gives me
the sense of "Groundhog Day" within progressive
circles. It feels as if the same discussion take places over and again. No matter what has transpired
in the intervening years; no matter what mass
struggles; no matter what theoretical insights; progressives find themselves debating the relative importance of electoral
politics and the pros and cons of specific candidates. These debates
frequently become nothing short of slugfests as charges are thrown
around of reformism, sell-outs and purism. And then, during the next
cycle, we are back at it.

What has struck me in the current cycle are two related but distinct problems. First, progressives have no national electoral strategy to speak of.
Second, elections cannot be viewed simply or even mainly within the
context of the pros and cons of specific candidates. In fact, with regard
to the latter, there are much bigger matters at stake that are frequently
obscured by the candidates themselves.

Let's begin in reverse order. In a recent exchange on Facebook I had with
a friend, he raised the point that Hillary Clinton holds some positions to
the right of Donald Trump. His, apparent, point was that in a final election, should it come down to Clinton vs. Trump, it would actually not
make much of a difference who won. Someone I do not know responded
to my friend by pointing out that Hitler was to the "left" of certain candidates as well and that the issue of intolerance needed to be the point
of focus.

Looking at the platform or views of a candidate reveals only part of the
equation. It gives one a sense of the candidate. What is just as important
are the social forces that have assembled around a particular candidate

and the direction of their motion. Let's go back to Hitler for a moment. Within the NSDAP (Nazi Party) there were forces on the left and the right, of course these terms being quite relative. The Brownshirts, otherwise known as the SA (Stormtroopers) proselytized in favor of a "national revolution" in Germany. Hitler and his SA supporters advocated some very radical solutions to the problems facing Germany. They consciously utilized left-wing symbolism (such as a red flag as background to the swastika) in order to appeal to the working class and other disgruntled forces crushed by the economy. They did this while promoting antisemitism and militarism. On June 30, 1934, after assuming power

and after cementing his alliance with the German military and major elements of the economic establishment, Hitler and the SS crushed the SA and any further discussion of a "national revolution." While the SA may have sincerely been interested in their perverted notion of a "national revolution," the Nazi movement had built a base and a set of alliances that was interested in something quite different: a radical restructuring of capitalism, the end of political democracy, and a relocation of Germany among the world's powers.

Right-wing populism, whether in its fascist or non-fascist form, can assume a posture and articulate a language that can appear left-wing. History has demonstrated this time and again. Yet right-wing populism is NOT "right-wing + populism" but is, instead, a specific integral phenomenon known as "right-wing populism." It is irrationalist, xenophobic, frequently anti-Semitic, racist and misogynistic. And it is a movement, rather than just a few crazed individuals.

Looking at Trump and his platform tells us something but not enough. An examination of his base and their objectives is just as important. The white revanchism that exists among his base, i.e., the politics of racial and imperial revenge, flows through and from the Trump campaign like waste through a sewer. The economic anger of the Trump base is something that is very real, but it is anger seen through a racial lens and articulated through coded racial language.

The Trump and Cruz forces, to broaden this discussion a bit, are not only intent on seizing the White House, but they also want to alter the entire political landscape. The work by the Right-wing at the local and state levels, in this regard, cannot be ignored. Efforts to promote the conditions for a Constitutional Convention have been underway for years by the right-wing, with a clear aim of overthrowing 20th century victories. This corresponds with, though is independent of, plans by candidates, such as Trump and Cruz, to eliminate various institutions, e.g., Department of Energy, Education, that are, at least in theory, to address broader popular needs.

For these reasons, the near exclusive focus on the individuals known as Trump and Cruz can be misleading. What is contained in their base? What does one make of the violence associated most especially with the Trump campaign? Neither of these campaigns, as idiotic as they may appear, are reality TV shows. These are spearheads of a social movement that is very deeply rooted in the settler colonialism and racism of U.S. society.

This brings us to the matter of the lack of a progressive electoral strategy. It is in large part because (a) progressives are very divided about the relative importance of electoral politics, and (b) because of our near exclusive focus on the candidates, that there is no coherent national progressive electoral strategy. This does not mean that people lack ideas. There are important forces out there ranging from the Working Families Party to the Progressive Democrats of America to more local formations such as New Virginia Majority and New Florida Majority that are articulating creative strategic approaches. Yet, this work is less than the sum of its parts (with no criticism implied of these groups). It is, however, the case that when most progressives think about electoral politics they think less about strategy and more about a particular candidacy or set of candidacies, more often than not candidacies that have not emerged out of the progressive movements.

A progressive electoral strategy begins with an assumption: that progressives are interested in not only conducting defensive battles, but actually winning power. This is a complicated assumption because there are many progressives who appear to not be particularly interested in winning power unless winning power means the death of capitalism, i.e., either capitalism dies or we sit back and criticize the system. Such views end up reinforcing cynicism but also pessimism about the ability to win any change. Constant defensive battles are demoralizing and disempowering.

Even for those of us who believe in system change and social transformation, there is a vital need for an interim approach, if only to address the dire needs of masses of people for basic survival (including matters relative to the environment). This need is a call for a fight for political power, and such a fight necessitates a strategy.

I frequently mention an experience I had in Texas about a year ago. I gave a talk about the political situation following which there were comments from the audience regarding the terrible political circumstances in Texas. I listened carefully and then asked the group: "How do we win power in Texas?" Well, the group was stunned. For many—I could tell—my question seemed to come out of nowhere and was over the top. Yet I went on to explain that progressives need to rethink the manner in which we approach our situation. Texas, for instance, is changing in many important respects, including demographically. Thus, the question I believe that we should be asking concerns the social movements in Texas, and which are key? I would also ask about the politics of different cities? Further, what alliances can and must be built? I would suggest that such questions need to be asked of every state in the USA.

A seriousness about winning power means, to borrow from Sun-Tzu, to know your enemy and know yourself. With respect to the fight for power, this means that we must understand the terrain in which we are operating; the nature of power in the USA; the nature of our enemies; the nature of both our tactical and strategic allies; and the growth and decline of various progressive social movements. Putting this together helps place progressives on a road towards winning rather than a road towards the glorious and heroic defeats with which too many of us are familiar.

Bill Fletcher, Jr. is a Senior Scholar with the Institute for Policy Studies, on the editorial board of BlackCommentator.com, the immediate past president of TransAfrica Forum, and the author of "They're Bankrupting Us" – And Twenty Other Myths about Unions. Follow him at www. billfletcherjr.com

Source URL: http://www.alternet.org/election-2016/why-progressives-need-national-electoral-strategy-and-fast

Links:

[1] http://www.alternet.org/authors/bill-fletcher-jr-0
[2] http://alternet.org
[3] http://www.billfletcherjr.com
[4] mailto:corrections@alternet.org?Subject=Typo on Why Progressives Need a National Electoral Strategy—and Fast
[5] http://www.alternet.org/
[6] http://www.alternet.org/%2Bnew_src%2B

Updating Our Strategy: Revisiting the U.S. 'Six Party System' Hypothesis

The two major parties in the U.S. are not ideological parties in the European sense, but are constantly changing coalitions. The only victory of a new 'First Party' came with the collapse of the Whigs, in 1860, pictured here.

By Carl Davidson
The Rag Blog

March 21, 2016 - Successful strategic thinking starts with gaining knowledge, particularly gaining adequate knowledge of the big picture; of all the political and economic forces involved... It's not a one-shot deal. Since both Heaven and Earth are always changing, strategic thinking must always be kept up to date, reassessed and revised.

This statement was part of the opening to a widely-circulated article I wrote about two years ago, "Strategic Thinking on the U.S. Six Party System." It's time to take my own advice, and reassess the working hypothesis I put forward back then.

For the most part, the strategic picture holds. I suggested setting aside the traditional "two party system" frame, which obscures far more than it reveals, and making use of a "six party" model instead. The new hypothesis, I suggested, had far more explanatory power regarding the events unfolding before us.

Some critics have objected to my use of the term "party" for what are really factional or interest group clusters. The point is taken, but I would also argue that U.S. major parties in general are not ideological parties in the European sense, but constantly changing coalitions of these clusters with no firm commitment to program or discipline. So I will continue to use "parties," but with the objection noted.

The "six parties," under two tents, were labeled as the Tea Party and the Multinationalists under the GOP tent, and the Blue Dogs, the Third Way New Democrats, the Old New Dealers, and the Congressional Progressive Caucus, under the Democratic tent. Most of these ran at least one presidential candidate as their voice — Bernie Sanders for the Congressional Progressive Caucus, Martin O'Malley for the Old New Dealers, Hillary Clinton for the Third Way, Jim Webb for the Blue Dogs, Jeb Bush and Marco Rubio for the Multinationalists, and a mixed bag under Tea Party (The GOP had 17 contenders starting off, and Hillary nearly hegemonic in the Democrats).

First and most important for us on the left was the rise of Bernie Sanders.

The changes, however, are important. Instead of four under the Dem tent and two under the GOP tent, we now have three under each. First and most important for us on the left was the rise of Bernie Sanders, who showed far more strength than imagined. Second was the dramatic and unexpected flowering of Trump and right-wing populism on the right. Both of these, from different directions, challenged, narrowed, and weakened the dominant neoliberal hegemonic bloc, which spanned both the GOP multinationals and the Third Way Democrats. Here's a new snapshot of the range of forces for today, starting from the left side:

The Rainbow Social Democrats. This is a better description than simply calling it the Congressional Progressive Caucus (CPC). It doesn't mean each leader active here is in a social-democrat group. It means the core of the CPC platform is roughly similar to the left social democrat groupings in Europe, and this is made even more evident with Bernie's self-description as a "democratic socialist."

It must be noted, however, that even though he's made the term "democratic socialist" more popular and acceptable, he's not running on socialism, but on a platform best described as a common front versus finance capital, war, and the right. This is true of groups like Die Linke ("The Left") in Germany as well. This is good, since it can unite more than a militant minority of actual socialists. Instead it's a platform that can also unite a progressive majority around both immediate needs and structural reforms, including both socialists and non-socialists.

For details, see Bernie's full platform at BernieSanders.com. Joining with Sanders in the Congressional Progressive Caucus, are PDA leaders such as Rep. Raul Grijalva of Arizona, Rep. Keith Ellison of Minnesota, and Rep Barbara Lee of California — all key voices giving the "party" a "rainbow" character.

It needs to be noted, though, that the Congressional Black Caucus, close overlapping ally of the Congressional Progressive Caucus, has largely gone over to Hillary and the Third Way grouping, with the result of only three out of 10 Black voters currently going for Sanders. Sanders does manage to win Latino voters by larger numbers. For example, all the Latino wards in Chicago on the second Super Tuesday went for Sanders, while the Black wards continued to be dominated by Clinton.

Apart from winning several primaries with a positive, high road approach, this party is noted for two things: first, the huge, elemental outpourings of young people, mainly students and the young workers of the distressed "precariat" sector of the class, in gigantic rallies and "Bernie marches"; and second, by an incredible online fundraising machine, involving some five million donors, making small donations every few weeks or months, that enables the campaign to continue to thrive without Super PACs' or other wealthy donors. This points the way for candidates of the left in the future at all levels.

The Keynesian Liberal-Labor Bloc. Previously called the Old New Dealers, this is a bit more accurate as a label. It's mainly the political action side of the AFL-CIO and their close allies in civil rights, women's and retiree groups, and several related think tanks like Campaign for America's Future. They are currently fence-sitting, after O'Malley made a bid for their support, but collapsed. Many among the leadership of their base organizations are leaning toward Hillary, while many below lean toward Bernie. Expect them to side with Clinton in the end, since she has been going all out with a "united front from above" approach to winning them to an alliance with her Third Way party.

Bernie has taken a 'united front from below' approach, aimed at the rank and file.

In similar fashion, Bernie has taken a "united front from below" approach, aimed at the rank-and-file, that has won over the Transit Workers, Nurses, and Postal Workers unions, and former leaders of the NAACP like Ben Jealous. Once this party with its union base does get into motion, however, it has a powerful get-out-the-vote and educational apparatus. It will face a special problem, however, in winning workers at the base away from Trump, who are estimated at as much as 33% of white workers, although some of these workers may also be more inclined toward Sanders than Clinton.

The Third Way New Democrats. Formed by the Clintons, with an international assist from Tony Blair and others, and funded by Wall Street finance capitalists, their founding idea was to move toward neoliberalism by "creating distance" between themselves and the traditional Left-Labor-Liberal bloc, the traditional unions and civil rights groups still connected to the New Deal legacy. Another part of the "Third Way" thinking was to shift the key social base away from the core of the working class to college-educated suburban voters, but keeping its alliances with Black and women's groups still functional.

Thus it tries to temper the harsher neoliberalism of the GOP by "triangulating" with neo-Keynesian policies. But the overall effect is to move Democrats generally rightward. While this has been Hillary Clinton's starting point, in the current campaign she has, piece by piece, adopted some positions, at least for the sake of campaigning, from both the Liberal-Labor bloc and the Rainbow Social Democrats to what she espouses in her stump speeches.

GOP turnout is up, while Democratic turnout is lackluster, save for Bernie rallies.

In terms of the current relation of forces, counting by delegates, Hillary currently has a two-to-one advantage over Bernie. The Third Way and allied groupings, however, are facing serious problems at the base. In many races, GOP turnout is up, while Democratic turnout is lackluster, save for Bernie rallies. Part of this is racialized, with 90% or more Blacks favoring either Clinton or Sanders, while white workers are split, as just noted, with as much as a third going to Trump and the GOP.

The Blue Dogs. This party has collapsed. Its presidential candidate, Jim Webb, dropped out after a few rounds in the debates where he gained little traction. He tried to combine pro-militarism with an anti-Iraq war stand. He then explored the prospects of a third party run, but recently held a press conference giving it up. He also indicated he was leaning toward Trump, which fits in with his Southern and Appalachian social base among military-industrial workers. The Blue Dogs may return at some point, but we still get "six parties" rather than five by new developments under the GOP tent, most importantly, the huge expansion and then division of the Tea Party into two parties.

The GOP Establishment. This is the name now widely used in the media for what we previously labeled the Multinationalists. It's mainly the upper crust and neoliberal business elites that have owned and run the GOP for years, allied with the smaller groups of neocons on foreign policy, and opposed by the anti-global neo-isolationist nationalism in a sector of the GOP base, i.e., the Tea Party. The Establishment also favored a U.S. hegemonist and unilateralist approach abroad, with many still defending the Bush-Cheney disaster in Iraq.

Their candidates were Jeb Bush and Marco Rubio, but when both of these collapsed under fire from Donald Trump, their voice is now reduced to that of John Kasich, governor of Ohio. Kasich presents himself as a pragmatic, pro-worker neoliberal, a difficult circle to square. Previously dominant in the GOP, the Establishment forces are now weakened by both sides of the Tea Party split, the Rightwing Populists under Trump and the Christian Nationalist Theocrats under Sen. Ted Cruz, who are currently both stronger in numbers than the "Establishment" party. They could be pushed out entirely by the time of the Cleveland convention, and formally split into two.

They present themselves as the only true, 'values-centered' (Biblical) conservatives.

The Christian Nationalist Theocrats. This is a subset of the former Tea Party made up of several Christian rightist trends, some simply conservative while others are theocracy-minded fundamentalists, especially the "Dominionist" sects of which Ted Cruz's father is active. They present themselves as the only true, "values-centered" (Biblical) conservatives. They argue against any kind of compromise with the "liberal-socialist bloc'" which ranges, in their view, from the GOP's Mitt Romney to Bernie Sanders.

They are more akin to classic liberalism than neoliberalism in economic policy, and thus stress abandoning nearly all regulations, much of the safety net, overturning Roe v. Wade, getting rid of marriage equality (in the name of "religious liberty") and abolishing the IRS and any progressive taxation in favor of a single flat tax. Effectively, it amounts to affirmative action for the better off, and the rise of the rich is supposed to pull everyone else upwards as well.

They do at times argue for neoisolationism on some matters, but favor an all-out holy war on "radical Islamic terrorism," to the point of "making the sand glow," and stand for ripping up Obama's recent agreements with Iran and Cuba. With Cruz as their leader, they have become the second most powerful grouping under the GOP tent, and the one with the most reactionary platform and outlook, even more so than Trump.

The Rightwing Populists. Starting as still another subset of the Tea Party, this "party" has mushroomed under the self-bankrolled Trump candidacy. Trump, an "outlier elite" in his own right, is now positioned either to win the GOP nomination outright, or have a plurality of enough militant delegates at the GOP convention that the nomination will be given to him on the first or second ballots, or as Trump puts it, "there will be riots." Given the fact that as many as one-third of the traditional GOP base is refusing to vote for Trump, with many willing to vote "third party" if one shapes up, and since they believe Hilary will defeat Trump anyway, the GOP, at this time, is thus effectively split into three warring parties.

The core outlook of Rightwing Populism is "producerism" vs "parasitism." Employed workers, business owners, real estate developers, small bankers are all "producers" and they oppose parasite groups above and below, but mainly those of "the Other" below them — the unemployed ("Get a Job!" as an epithet), the immigrants, poor people of color, Muslims, and more. Trump entered politics by declaring Obama to be an illegal alien and an illegitimate office holder (a parasite above), but quickly shifted to Mexicans and Muslims and anyone associated with "Black Lives Matter."

Trump's favored outlook has deep roots in American history.

Trump's favored outlook has deep roots in American history, from the anti-Indian ethnic cleansing of President Andrew Jackson, to the nativism of the Know Nothings, to the lynch terror of the KKK, to the anti-elitism of George Wallace and the Dixiecrats. Internationally, he combines aggressive jingoism, threats of trade wars, and an isolationist "white nationalism" aimed at getting others abroad to fight your battles for you. Trump's success, however, also contains his weakness: the support of distressed white workers. At present, they are forming the social basis of his victories, assuming they will get lush jobs with his 'Make America Great Again!' promises. The problem is, Trump has no programs. He only has hot buttons he pushes, but when it comes to spelling out an actual program and how any promise would be implemented and funded, he's always the artful dodger. This creates an unstable class contradiction in his operation, one bound to surface as promises are unfulfilled. What does it all mean?

With this brief descriptive and analytical mapping of the upper crust of American politics, many things begin to fall in place. The subaltern groupings in the GOP have risen in revolt against the losses imposed on them by the neoliberal Establishment of the Romneys and the Bushes.

Ironically, this is "the chickens coming home to roost," since the GOP Establishment has encouraged and funded these "New Right" alliances ever since Ronald Reagan's and Richard Nixon's "Southern Strategy" and its appeal to the base of George Wallace.

But they could never deliver the goods to right-wing workers. They were still, after all, workers, who saw themselves sinking or stagnating under the harsh neoliberalism of the right. Now, even though they have rebelled and flocked to a "Great Leader," one whose rule would deepen every crisis and conflict facing the country, they are social dynamite.

On the other hand, the Hillary Clinton candidacy, seeking a "continuation" of the Obama administration, represents, at its core, an alliance between the "Third Way" and the Keynesian Labor Liberals, while holding out an olive branch to the Rainbow Social Democrats as an energetic but critical secondary ally.

The Sanders campaign, and its allied groupings, the Progressive Democrats of America and the Working Families Party, are still likely to soldier on to the convention, doing as much grassroots organizing along the way as they can. They have few illusions about Clinton's leftward shift, and are well aware that campaigning is one thing, while governing is another. So they continue to press all their issues and policies of a common front vs finance capital, war, and the right, building more and more clout as they go.

This "big picture" also reveals much about the current budget debates, which are shown to be three-sided — the extreme austerity neoliberalism of all three parties under the GOP tent, the "austerity lite" budget of the Third Way-dominated Senate Democrats, and the left Keynesian, progressive and social democratic "Back to Work" budget of the Rainbow Social Democrats and the Congressional Progressive Caucus. The "Keynesian Labor Liberals" remain caught in the middle, often holding decent programs as positions, but not willing to do much to fight for them, looking for safe ways "to go with the winner" and accept "half a loaf."

The far right has grown in strength and virulence.

All this shows why and how Hillary Clinton or Bernie Sanders would likely be able to pull together a majority electoral coalition. But it also reveals why either of them might still be thwarted in pulling together an effective governing coalition in 2017, (assuming they are able to defeat Trump or Cruz). The far right has grown in strength and virulence, while the "regular" conservative right has grown in intransigence. They still hold the House and the Senate, though this may change a bit in November, but Congress will still be an obstacle to any Democrat in the White House.

The old Establishment, led by Kasich at this point, is likely to be out in the cold, unless they shift over to Hillary, which a few are already talking about. All the parties of the GOP right, especially the ones on top, need to be crushed in November 2016. Both Clinton and Sanders have strengths and weaknesses, but Sanders would likely be the stronger candidate, given the historic scandals and anti-worker policies of the Clintons. Trump has already warned that he will use every piece of mud he can find to sling in her direction.

Finally, there is the one major positive factor that was barely conceivable only two years ago: the dramatic youth insurgency behind the only socialist in Congress. No longer on the margins, Sanders has both widened the legitimacy of socialism and put anti-finance capital, antiwar, and anti-fascist proposals at the center of the country's political discussion, and to audiences of tens of millions.

It didn't come from nowhere, but can be best seen as a reemergent Occupy 4.0, following the original Occupy 1.0 explosion of protest against the Banksters, to Black Lives Matter and the Fight for 15 insurgencies (2.0), to the Climate Justice mobilizations (3.0). These are all elemental risings of the "precariat," the young and stressed out and underemployed and debt-ridden sector of the working class and the oppressed generally, as a critical force in society calling on the main force, "the 99%," to activate itself and enter the battleground.

In summary, here are a few things to keep in mind. If you decide to intervene in electoral work to build independent working class grassroots organizations, you don't go "inside the Democratic Party." There's not much of an "inside" there anymore. Most of what is left are small groups of lawyers, fundraisers, and media consultants clustered tightly around each incumbent.

What you do instead is join or work with one of the two factions/"parties" that are left-of-center under its tent. Your aim is to make either of these stronger, preferably Rainbow Social Democrats. Then to shift the overall balance of forces, your task is to defeat the Rightwing Populists, the Christian Nationalist Theocrats, and the Establishment GOP while expanding the Congressional Progressive Caucus. But you want to do this in a way that builds your organizational clout and influence under the Democratic tent at the expense of the Third Way.

Strategically, we want to build a growing force along the class and democratic fault lines under that tent until it is stretched to the ripping point.

Even in the short run, the balance of forces needs altering in favor of the left. At present, not a single piece of progressive legislation is going to get passed without a major shift in this direction, and that would require growing a new counter-hegemonic bloc inside and outside of the Democratic tent, and at all levels of government.

We are interested in pushing the popular front vs. finance capital to its limits.

We have to keep in mind, however, that "shifting the balance of forces" is mainly an indirect and somewhat ephemeral gain. It does "open up space," but for what? Progressive initiatives matter for sure, but much more is required strategically. We are interested in pushing the popular front vs. finance capital to its limits, and within that effort, developing a 21st century socialist bloc.

If that comes to scale in the context of a defeat of the right, the "Democratic Tent" is also likely to collapse and implode, given the sharper class contractions and other fault lines that lie within it, much as the Whigs did in the 19th Century. That demands an ability to regroup all the progressive forces there and on the outside into a new "First Party" alliance, one that also includes a militant minority of socialists, which will be able to contend for power.

Strategy Needs Tactics

An old classic formula summing up the strategic thinking of the united front is appropriate here: "Unite and develop the progressive forces, win over the middle forces, isolate and divide the backward forces, then crush our adversaries one by one." In short, we have to have a policy and set of tactics for each one of these elements, as well as a strategy for dealing with them overall. Moreover, take note of warning from the futurist Alvin Toffler: "If you don't have a strategy, you're part of someone else's strategy." Then finally, as to tactics, "wage struggle on just grounds, to our advantage and with restraint."

To conclude, we still need to start with a realistic view of ourselves as an organized socialist left. We are quite small as organizations, but now we can see we are swimming in a sea of millions open to socialism. What can we do now? In brief, set up Jacobin/In These Times reading groups in your living rooms and unite socialists with them, join or start PDA or WFP chapters everywhere, use organizations and broad "Third Reconstruction" alliances and popular rainbow assemblies to build mass mobilizations and win elections, with both socialists and Rainbow progressives, starting at the base, focused on city and state governments, and expanding the Congressional Progressive Caucus. You rarely gain victories at the top that have not been won and consolidated earlier at the base.

Most of all, in order to form broader and winning coalitions, you need organizations of your own to form coalitions and alliances WITH! Seize the time and Git 'er done!

Read more articles by Carl Davidson on The Rag Blog and listen to Thorne Dreyer's five Rag Radio interviews with Carl.

Carl Davidson, a longtime activist and author, is national co-chair of Committees of Correspondence for Democracy and Socialism, is on the national board of Solidarity Economy Network, is active with Progressive Democrats of America, and is a member of Local 3657 of the United Steel Workers. A former vice-president and national secretary of Students for a Democratic Society (SDS) and news editor at the Guardian (U.S.), Carl lives in Western Pennsylvania.

We Need You To Join Us....

We're inviting you to join the Committees of Correspondence for Democracy and Socialism. We need your help in building a progressive majority for peace, justice and equality—and then pushing on to a new society where these will be the rule, rather than the exception. Socialism is being more widely discussed today than any time since the 1960s, and you can't take part in it fully without a socialist organization.

Working with many others, CCDS aims to end existing wars and prevent new ones. We oppose the current austerity being imposed upon the working people, a burden made even heavier by militarism and the hidden costs of non-renewable energy systems. We need a global order based on peaceful relations among nations, mutual respect and human rights, and the creation of economies that can exist in harmony with nature.

You can make a difference. Lend a hand in organizing with others to fight for a progressive agenda in the streets, workplaces, communities of faith and schools. It's not crowded up front, so sign up today!

Fill out and mail today.

_____ Yes, I'd like to join the CCDS. Enclosed is my check for:
$ _____.
   I'd like a subscription to Dialogue & Initiative. Enclosed is my check for $12.50 (Non-Members, $15.00).
   I know good causes need money. Here is my contribution of $_____.

Name _____
Address _____
City _____ State _____ Zip _____
Phone_____ Email _____

Make check payable to Committees of Correspondence, and mail to: CCDS Membership, 6422 Irwin Ct., Oakland, CA, 94609

Email: national@cc-ds.org Web: www.cc-ds.org

The Committees of Correspondence for Democracy and Socialism (CCDS) is a national organization dedicated to the struggle for justice, equality, democracy, peace and socialism. The annual membership is $36 for individuals; $18 for unemployed, seniors, youth, and others with low income; $48 for households

www.ingramcontent.com/pod-product-compliance
Lightning Source LLC
Chambersburg PA
CBHW032005170526
45157CB00002B/548